INSIGHT GUIDES

EXPLORE

SHANGHAI

CONTENTS

ARCHITECTURE

Shanghai is a city with a fabulous range of architecture, from wonderful Art Deco (routes 5 and 6) to lane houses (route 6) and dramatic modern skyscrapers (route 11).

RECOMMENDED ROUTES FOR...

ART ENTHUSIASTS

The main draw is the inspirational M50 Art District (route 9). For a more systematic viewing, art fans will want to see the Power Station of Art and the China Art Palace (route 11), which showcase the country's high-profile modern art scene.

CHILDREN

Across the river from the city centre, the Pudong district (route 11) has a cluster of child-friendly attractions. Kids will also enjoy trips out of town to the gardens of Suzhou (route 14) and the beautiful 'water town' of Tongli (route 13).

FOOD AND DRINK

There is a vast range to choose from in what is one of the world's great culinary centres. Try authentic local food in the Old City (route 5), or refined international dining on the Bund (route 1).

MUSEUMS

The Shanghai Museum on People's Square (route 3) is a great place to learn about China's long history, while the Jewish Refugees Museum (route 8) is well worth going out of your way to see.

PARKS AND GARDENS

People's Park (route 3) and Fuxing Park (route 7) provide welcome green space, while further afield Suzhou and Hangzhou (routes 14 and 15) are famed for their classical gardens.

SHOPPING

Nanjing Road West (route 4) is famous for its luxury shops, while to the south are Xintiandi and Huaihai Road (routes 6 and 7). The Ming-style bazaar in the Old City (route 5), Tianzifang (route 7) and M50 Art District (route 9) are great for souvenirs.

TEMPLES

The colourful Jade Buddha Temple (route 9) and classical Longhua Pagoda (route 10) are highlights, while Xiahai Temple (route 8) feels utterly authentic.

INTRODUCTION

An introduction to Shanghai's geography, customs and culture, plus illuminating background information on cuisine, history and what to do when you're there.

The Oriental Pearl Tower

EXPLORE SHANGHAI

Bold, brash Shanghai is China's glamour city, where the faded glory of its treaty port history exists hand-in-glove with a soaring skyline and a brilliant future. Prepare to be dazzled.

Spoil of the Opium Wars, Shanghai was opened to trade in 1842 and subsequently carved up into concessions by foreigners from around the world – an experiment that gave the city its global soul, its thirst for progress and its knack for international commerce. However, such foreign dominance also created a cauldron for resentment, and the Chinese Communist Party held its first meeting here in 1921. Revolution marched alongside old Shanghai's decadent ways, finally winning over the city in May 1949. Since the beginning of the era of 'reform and opening up' in 1978, Shanghai has been on a vast growth trajectory, transforming its skyline and economy, building, booming and innovating. The result? A truly global city for the 21st century.

The routes in this book, arranged geographically, take in the different parts of the multilayered Shanghai story – old and new, international and Chinese, business and cultural.

NAVIGATING THE CITY

Shanghai borders the East China Sea to the east, Hangzhou Bay to the south, and the provinces of Jiangsu and Zhejiang to the west. The limits of this maritime city's neighbourhoods are also defined by its waterways; the Huangpu River separates Shanghai's newest district, Pudong ('east of the Huangpu') from the rest of the city, Puxi ('west of the Huangpu', pronounced 'poo-shee'). The Suzhou Creek divides Puxi's thriving heart from its quieter northern suburbs.

Shanghai Municipality covers roughly 6,340 sq km (2,450 sq miles), within which lie its 17 districts. New district boundaries have been drawn, but the shape and feel of the old foreign settlements and Nanshi ('the old Chinese City') are still discernible. Streets run north to south and east to west in grid-like fashion, except for oval-shaped Nanshi, which follows the lines of the old city wall, and People's Square, defined by the ghost of the old racetrack. The major streets run the length of the city and have directional tags: Huaihai Road West, Central and East, for example. Buildings are usually numbered sequentially (but not always); odd numbers on one side of the street and even numbers on the

Jade Buddha Temple lanterns

Getting a good view of Pudong

other; the numbering on residential lanes *(longtang)* that run off the main streets bears no relation to the main street numbering.

The 98km (61-mile) outer ring road, the A20, takes a lap outside the city limits, while the inner ring Zhongshan Road loops around the perimeter of Puxi and Pudong, changing its name in Pudong and east Hongkou before turning back into Zhongshan Road. The city is bisected from east to west by the Yan'an Road Elevated Highway. Crossing the Huangpu River to Pudong from Puxi can be done via ferry, metro, 12 bridges including Nanpu, Yangpu and Lupu, or 13 tunnels.

Street signs are written in pinyin romanisation (or in some cases, in English) and Chinese characters, but most locals and taxi drivers know streets only by their Chinese names. Public transport is modern, clean, efficient and wide-reaching. It's also fairly accessible for foreigners in that most signage and announcements are in both Chinese and English (bus stop signs are the one exception). However, very little English is spoken by drivers and other transport workers.

HISTORY AND ARCHITECTURE

Shanghai's history stretches back to the year 751, when Huating County was officially recognised. By 1292, the central government had estab-lished Shanghai County, acknowledged as a direct ancestor of contemporary Shanghai. The character of Shanghai as we know it today, however, was most profoundly shaped in the aftermath of the first Opium War in 1842. The treaty that ended that war divided the city into international concessions and brought in a cosmopolitan mix of traders, adventurers and people from around the world fleeing from poverty, revolution and war. Fortunes were made (and lost), and Shanghai began to develop the glamorous sheen and business acumen that it retains today. For key dates see page 24.

Soaring skyline

This influx also exerted a profound influence on the city's built environment. Architects from China and around the world created buildings in international styles. Neoclassical, Tudor Revival, Mediterranean, Italianate and most notably Art Deco all feature in Shanghai's landscape. Even the city's domestic *longtang* lanes and *shikumen* houses are an East–West hybrid, unique to Shanghai (see page 22).

Shanghai's economic rise since the mid-1990s echoes the 1930s boom with a brand-new skyline and a particular fondness for skyscrapers. The city has thousands of high-rises, with thousands more planned, and three of the world's 12 tallest buildings rise up proudly (the Shanghai Tower, World Financial Centre and Jinmao Tower).

Shoppers pose for pictures in Xintandi

CLIMATE

Shanghai's northern subtropical monsoon climate means plenty of rainfall during the summer months, and four distinct seasons: a hot, humid summer; a damp, cold winter; and crisp, if brief, spring and autumn, which are the best times to visit (see page 119).

THE SHANGHAINESE

Shanghai's population of 23 million is made up of 14.12 million registered Shanghai residents and a further 9 million with household registrations outside the city. The city's burgeoning expatriate population – more than 164,000 from around the world – lends the city a vibrantly cosmopolitan feel.

Shanghainese are considered to be smart, hip – and a little arrogant. The men have a reputation for being shrewd businessmen, but docile at home – Shanghai men famously, uncomplainingly, carry their girlfriends' handbags. The women are just as sharp as the men when it comes to business, and very well turned out. Impressions count a great deal here: visitors from Beijing chuckle that even the undersides of the city's elevated highways are painted. Shanghainese are conspicuous consumers, with a passion for upmarket brands, luxury cars and fine dining. The city's history of amalgamating East and West gave rise to a style called *hai pai*, which translates today to an openness to Western ideas and customs.

LOCAL CUSTOMS

Shanghai has a relentless big-city pace, rising early and going to bed late. By 7am, the tai chi practitioners and ballroom dancers are going through their paces in the parks, and the markets are buzzing. Offices, banks and museums are open by 9am, while shops open between 10 and 11am, and restaurants begin serving lunch by 11.30am.

Shanghai has a lively nightlife scene, and the city's bars and clubs keep going well into the early hours, with some remaining open all night.

Speaking English

The city has the largest population of English-speakers in the country, yet there are still numerous situations in which very little English is spoken – these include taxis, markets, shopping centres, public transport (though the signs are bilingual), police, local hospitals (though some have a 'foreigners' section') and some government offices. In most public places, however, you will probably find English-speaking locals, who are usually happy to help.

Besides an English newspaper (*Shanghai Daily*) and a TV channel with 24-hour English and Japanese programmes, there is also a service hotline (tel: 962288) with 15 languages to assist foreigners in Shanghai.

Futuristic Shanghai   *Playing Chinese chess in People's Park*

DON'T LEAVE SHANGHAI WITHOUT...

Strolling along the Bund. Take a leisurely wander along Shanghai's iconic waterfront promenade admiring the historic stone edifices of the former 'Wall Street of Asia'. Take the obligatory snap of the futuristic towers that face-off across the river then retire to one of the Bund's glam restaurants or bars. Our pick: The Long Bar or M on the Bund terrace. See page 28.

Taking in sky-high views. Ascend one of Pudong's glittering skyscrapers (see page 71) for vertiginous views across the vast metropolis. The 100-storey glass-bottom bridge atop the Shanghai World Financial Centre is presently the city's tallest.

Discovering Chinese contemporary art. Check out the cutting edge of Chinese contemporary art at M50 art district beside Suzhou Creek, filled with small galleries and working artist studios. See page 65.

Experiencing Shanghai's legendary nightlife. Shanghai is at its best after dark. Don your glad rags and join the all-night party at one of the glamorous cocktail lounges or clubs along the Bund (see page 77). Or visit a live jazz bar (see page 117) – the soundtrack to Shanghai's 1930s golden age.

Exploring atmospheric old lanes and heritage villas. Despite the onslaught of high-rise development, Shanghai has managed to hold onto many of its old neighbourhoods. Lively residential lanes lined with traditional *shikumen* houses remain in areas around Nanjing Road West (see page 42) and the former French Concession (see page 52). Here, you can also visit the well-preserved former residences of luminaries such as Sun Yat-Sen, Zhou Enlai and Soong Qingling (see page 52).

Revving through the lanes in a sidecar motorcycle. There's no more thrilling way to explore Shanghai's colourful neighbourhoods than by vintage sidecar motorcycle. Shanghai Insiders (see page 128) offers narrated tours of the city in a Changjiang 750cc, a replica of the Russian Ural sidecar that was formerly used by China's People's Liberation Army.

Daytripping through classical Chinese landscapes. Hangzhou (see page 86) and Suzhou (see page 82) are famed throughout China for their idyllic gardens and lakes. High-speed road and rail links mean that both are easily accessed from Shanghai.

Chowing down on local dumplings. Shanghai's dumplings are justly famous. Savour the juicy steamed *xiaolongbao* at Din Tai Fung or Nanxiang (see page 112) and the hearty, pan-fried *shengjianbao* at Yang's Dumpling (see page 107). Bite carefully as they are filled with scalding broth!

Getting a grasp on past and future. A visit to the excellent Shanghai Museum is a great way to learn about Shanghai's long history and put the modern city into some sort of context. Close by, the Urban Planning Centre gives a view on what's still to come. See page 38.

Animal statue in the Shanghai Museum

POLITICS AND ECONOMICS

Shanghai is known for sending its politicians on to bigger jobs in Beijing. Jiang Zemin and Zhu Rongji are both former mayors who went on to become president and premier respectively. Xi Jinping, a former Shanghai Communist Party Secretary – the top-ranked position – is now the General Secretary of the CPC Central Committee.

China's financial capital

Shanghai is China's beating economic heart, and its financial capital. It is also the location for China's first free trade zone, which was launched in September 2013, part of a state-planned agenda for the city to be a fully-fledged global financial centre by 2020. With just 0.06% of the nation's land area, Shanghai still manages to contribute more than four percent of China's GDP.

Per capita GDP in 2012 was RMB85,373 (around USD14,120 at early 2014 exchange rates), on a par with a medium-sized developed country. In recent years, the city has witnessed unprecedented economic expansion in tandem with impressive infrastructure development – much of which was completed in time to host the record-breaking 2010 World Expo. Even as the pace slows as the national economy matures, GDP still increased by 7.5 percent in 2012. Overall optimism continues and consumer spending is strong; with retail sales rising 8.8 percent in 2012, and 8.7 percent in the first 10 months of 2013.

The government's massive investments during the 2008 financial crisis and Expo kept the Shanghai economy vibrant, but recognising that a more sustainable model was needed to the long-term, it is now focused on the transition to a consumption-driven economy even at the cost of lower GDP growth rate. The second area of long-term focus is the movement from being the world's factory – ie manufacturing – to a more creative, or innovation-oriented society: from 'Made in China' to 'Invented in China'. These transitions will help the government achieve its goal of becoming an international economic, financial, trade and shipping center by 2020.

Hand-in-hand with the economic policies designed to assure a well-off society, the government is also working to accelerate social development with the focus of improving livelihoods. To date, they have provided 17 million square metres of low-income housing, and the average living space of urban residents has been improved to 17 square metres. More resources have been invested in community nursing services for the elderly, and significant reform of the city's medi-care system is on the way.

What this means for the visitor is that Shanghai offers luxuries that few other Chinese cities can afford, with rates to match. Top-end hotels and restaurants

In Yuyuan Garden   *Girls in Qing Dynasty attire showing tea art at a festival*

command international price tags – and these are now being targeted more and more at the increasingly wealthy domestic market.

TOP TIPS FOR VISITING SHANGHAI

Getting around. Most taxi drivers in Shanghai speak no English so it's a good idea to carry the names of the places you want to visit written in English, pinyin and Chinese characters (the Chinese characters for the driver, the English for you, and the pinyin so you can confirm phonetically what the driver is saying). Your hotel concierge should be able to help.

Addresses. As many of the streets in Shanghai are very long, it is best to know the closest cross street to your destination – taxi drivers will be grateful.

Kids' entry prices. Ticket prices for children are most often determined by height, rather than age – if they're under 1.4m (4.6ft), they'll pay the reduced rate.

Maps. Free tourist maps of Shanghai in English are available at the airport (pick one up before you reach Customs) and at concierge desks of most hotels.

ATMs. International credit cards and bankcards (Cirrus, Plus, Visa, MasterCard, American Express) can be used to withdraw local currency from the ATMs of Chinese and foreign banks, which are easily found throughout the city.

Mobile SIM cards. To avoid roaming charges, get a pre-paid SIM card with a local number and fixed number of minutes. Many phone providers, hotels, convenience stores and self-serve kiosks at airports sell them in denominations of RMB100.

Theatre tickets. For a detailed list of arts and cultural performances in Shanghai, check out www.culture.sh.cn. You can book tickets via the website hotline (6217 2426) or directly with the venue.

Airports. Check your air ticket carefully as Shanghai has two airports: Pudong International Airport (30km east of city – code PVG) is mainly for international flights. Hongqiao Airport (15km west of city – SHA) is for domestic flights and some Hong Kong, Taiwan and South Korean routes.

French Concession walking tours. Shanghai's historic preservation group, Historic Shanghai (info@historic-shanghai.com), leads a monthly walking tour of the former French Concession. Led by Chinese-speaking historians and sinologists, the tours take you into homes, courtyards and hidden lanes to meet the locals and reveal layers of Shanghai's fascinating history.

Train timetable. High-speed trains tend to be most convenient for short-haul travel within China. Train timetables in English can be found at Travel China Guide (www.travelchinaguide.com/china-trains), which also has a handy app called China Trains that enables ticket bookings. 'G' trains are the fastest.

Huangpu ferry. A fun way to cross the river between Puxi and Pudong is via a local ferry. It costs just RMB2 and the views are priceless.

Traditional Chinese teapot

FOOD AND DRINK

Whether you're after an early-morning breakfast of crispy fried crullers or a late-night snack of plump steamed dumplings, you've come to the right place – Shanghai is a city that loves to eat 24 hours a day.

For sheer variety alone, Shanghai is one of the best places to eat in the whole of China. Dining choices range from miniature hole-in-the-wall eateries, where you squat on tiny stools to slurp your meal from plastic bowls, to swanky restaurants helmed by global culinary stars.

Over the past decade, famous chefs have poured in from around the world, transforming Shanghai into an international dining destination. The diversity is breathtaking, with culinary treats on offer from Africa, Brazil, India, Europe and Southeast Asia. There's also an impressive array of Chinese regional cuisines – from Yunnan to Xinjiang and Guangdong to Dongbei – plus, of course, plenty of Shanghai's own oily-sweet fare.

When to eat

A word of advice: Traditionally, Chinese mealtimes are on the early side, with dinner eaten around 6pm or 6.30pm. As a result, kitchens at Chinese restaurants tend to close early too, with mobile kebab grills and noodle stands materialising to cater to the late-night crowds. There are exceptions, though – Cantonese diner Cha's, Taiwanese Chamant and French supperclub Mr & Mrs Bund carry on serving into the early hours (see page 105).

SHANGHAINESE CUISINE

Throughout most of China's history, Shanghai was a muddy fishing village, while nearby cities such as Hangzhou and Nanjing, both former capitals of China, were famous for their beauty, culture, sophistication and fine food. Without any great palaces or emperors to inspire its cuisine, the Shanghainese instead turned to the bays and estuaries of the Yangtze Delta for their daily meals. Authentic local cuisine still relies heavily on freshwater crabs, eels, river fish and shrimps, along with traditional Chinese staples of chicken and pork, and a rich selection of seasonal local vegetables.

With its country roots, the preparation of Shanghainese cuisine is far less complex than that of its Cantonese or Beijing cousins, relying on soy sauce, oil and sugar for flavour, and featuring just three major methods of preparation: *hong shao* or red-cooked (with

Making noodles *Crayfish at a shopping mall buffet*

sugar and soy sauce), stewed or simply stir-fried with ginger and spring onions. One of the city's most iconic dishes is *hong shao* pork, fatty cubes of pork belly stewed in a soy sauce marinade until they practically melt in the mouth.

Shanghai's famous flair is better revealed in its cold dishes. Expect artistically arranged hors d'œuvres of dazzling variety, from plates of julienned vinegary pickles or tiny live shrimps served in rice wine, to spiced broad beans, 'drunken' chicken marinated in wine, and sweet wheat gluten *(kao fu)*.

As diners become more and more health-conscious, modern Shanghainese cuisine is starting to veer away from its overly dark and oily origins, and dishes at upscale Shanghai restaurants are less fatty and sweet than they once were. Meanwhile, the city is also starting to embrace the more sophisticated cuisine of the Jiangnan region (literally, south of the Yangtze River, encompassing Hangzhou, Suzhou, Ningbo and other surrounding cities), which is lighter and brighter, with more of a reliance on freshness and quick cooking.

Vegetarians can find dining in regular Chinese restaurants a challenge, as even vegetable dishes tend to be cooked in meat stock or contain small bits of meat. However, a number of Buddhist restaurants, such as Vegetarian Lifestyle (Zaozi Shu), offer large menus of meat-free Chinese dishes, often using tofu and mushrooms in ingenious ways to mimic typical meat dishes.

There's also an emerging trend toward vegetarian fine dining at elegant venues like Fuhe Hui.

Street food and dumplings

Shanghai dumplings are the city's favourite street food snack, and streetside stands are easily identified by their cylindrical bamboo steamers emitting fragrant puffs of steam.

Shanghai boasts two signature dumpling specialities: *shengjian mantou* are pan-fried in giant, crusty black pans. Filled with pork and scalding broth with crispy bottoms, they are also known by their English nickname, 'potstickers'. *Xiaolongbao* are smaller, more delicate steamed dumplings that look like translucent money pouches and are filled with pork, broth and,

Magic markets

Eating in Shanghai is still refreshingly defined by the seasons, and the city's fresh produce markets and corner fruit stores are the go-to places for raw ingredients. These lively neighbourhood markets are far removed from the bland supermarket experience – be prepared to encounter just-plucked vegetables with muddy roots, huge sides of pork, and still-splashing fish. Seasonal favourites to look out for include fat bamboo shoots in spring, *yangmei* berries and juicy white peaches in summer, and sweet miniature mandarins in winter.

Crabs are a perennial local favourite

sometimes, luxurious crab roe. The best places to sample *xiaolongbao* are at Din Tai Fung and Nan Xiang, while Yang's Fry Dumplings sizzles up the finest potstickers.

Breakfast is almost always eaten on the run, with *youtiao*, a long fried doughnut (or cruller), washed down with freshly brewed soybean milk, a local favourite. For the Shanghainese version of a breakfast burrito, try a *jianbing* pancake filled with fried egg, a crispy bean curd sheet, coriander and chilli sauce, cooked on a steaming griddle and rolled up for takeaway. Steamed *baozi* bread rolls are also eaten from big bamboo steamers, with a choice of fillings including pork, vegetables or sweet red bean paste.

Snacks and street food are available on virtually every corner in Shanghai, but the best selection can be found at Yu Garden Bazaar, where hordes of Chinese tourists patiently wait in line to sample the treats on offer. As well as those mentioned above, you can't miss the stench of another local favourite – *chou doufu*, or smelly bean curd. These little deep-fried cubes of fermented bean curd from Fenxian County on the outskirts of Shanghai are a somewhat acquired taste, but locals love their pungent flavour, especially when dipped in chilli sauce.

Hairy crabs

Arguably Shanghai's best-loved seasonal gourmet delicacy is the hairy crab. Every year from mid-October to the end of December, when the crabs are ripe with milt or roe, huge crowds of people drive to the shores of nearby Yangcheng Lake to catch and eat these critters, so named because of their down-covered claws. The crabs are also available in restaurants and markets across Shanghai, where they are steamed and served with a sauce of ginger, vinegar and sugar. Although no bigger than a human fist and very fiddly to eat, their meat and roe are sweet and buttery, with a rich flavour and superb velvety texture. Hairy crabs are considered to be 'cooling' to the body, so sherry-like Shaoxing wine is served to rebalance the body's yin and yang.

UNRIVALLED DINING SCENE

Shanghai's international culinary scene is so spectacular that the city had five restaurants appear on S. Pellegrino's inaugural 'Asia's 50 Best Restaurants' list in 2013, including Mr & Mrs Bund and Ultraviolet at Nos. 7 and 8.

Shanghai is a city of immigrants, and its restaurants represent a veritable microcosm of China. Along with the

---

Food and Drink Prices

Throughout this book, price guide for a two-course meal for one, with a drink:

$$$ = over RMB 250
$$ = RMB 100–250
$ = RMB 50–150

Dinner with a view   *Dumplings in bamboo steamers*

major cuisines – Cantonese, Beijing, Sichuan – are endless variations in between. Sichuan hotpot *(huoguo)* restaurants, at which a pot of chilli-laced bubbling soup sitting over a flame, is used for dipping and cooking vegetables and meats, are popular during the cold winters, as is Cantonese dim sum for an elegant brunch or high tea.

Due to long working days and small home kitchens, local residents generally prefer to eat out for most meals. Good restaurants tend to be packed at mealtimes, so book ahead or be prepared to wait. Food cleanliness and 'fake' ingredients are a genuine concern at some places, so be sure to stick to the more popular or recommended restaurants and food stalls, and be aware that you are probably getting what you pay for at very cheap dives.

Café culture

Café culture has a long heritage in Shanghai, and between classical Chinese teahouses and the European-influenced coffee shops and bakeries, there is a wealth of unique cafés for a reviving cuppa and people-watching. When you've had your fill of noodles, café chains such as Wagas and Element Fresh have multiple stores around the city offering fresh salads and good coffee, plus free WiFi access.

Shanghai's teahouses serve some of the finest teas in the world. Two of the most popular brews are *longjing* (Dragon Well) green tea from the hills of nearby Hangzhou, and rich black *pu'er* tea from Yunnan province. The *longjing* tea is mild, sweet and refreshing, while *pu'er* is rich, black and fully fermented, with an intensely smoky taste and a pronounced caffeine kick.

Local brews

Chinese beer is cheap and popular, with Tsingtao a reliable light pilsner. Sometimes people in Shanghai will drink *huang jiu*, or yellow wine, a sweet, golden-amber liquid made from glutinous rice. The best *huang jiu* comes from nearby Shaoxing. A more lethal beverage is *bai jiu*, or Chinese white liquor. Consumed from small glasses generally as a shot after a toast of '*gan bei*' (cheers), this transparent distilled grain spirit has a 40–60 percent alcohol content and is an acquired taste.

Grape wine is rapidly gaining popularity too. China is one of the world's biggest importers of wine, but now a handful of local Chinese wineries, such as Grace Vineyards, are producing some excellent home-grown vintages. A good sommelier will be able to recommend the best Chinese wines – the cheaper bottles are not recommended. Many upscale restaurants, bars and hotels have truly impressive cellars stocked with a global selection of wines. In Shanghai, the most expensive grands crus regularly get popped in a show of extravagance.

A Cultural Revolution–era poster at Dongtai Road Antique Market

SHOPPING

Shanghai is a shoppers' paradise. You can find almost anything in the city's plentiful markets, malls and boutiques, from traditional items such as fine tea, porcelain and Art Deco antiques to the latest fashions and contemporary art.

Shopping in Shanghai was once limited to cheap knock-offs and kitschy souvenirs, but now big-name global luxury brands are courting the city's new wealthy classes with opulent flagship stores and China-inspired product lines. Louis Vuitton opened its first China Maison and largest Shanghai store across four levels at Plaza 66, while New York 'Jeweller to the Stars' Harry Winston unveiled its largest global salon in a freestanding pavilion at Xintiandi.

Local designers and niche labels are also getting in on the act, taking advantage of the dominant consumer spirit and easy access to raw materials to launch an array of exciting new brands and boutiques. These can be found dotted around the former French Concession and the streets near the Bund.

Add to this traditional arts and crafts shops, antiques markets with one-off finds, and the city's famous custom tailors and silk purveyors ready to whip up a bespoke wardrobe, and you might want to consider bringing along an extra suitcase for your Shanghai purchases – or buying one, of course.

Shanghai's main shopping streets are Nanjing Road and Huaihai Road.

The eastern pedestrianised end of Nanjing Road is usually mobbed by local and out-of-town Chinese shoppers at weekends, while Nanjing Road West and Huaihai Road are studded with marble malls, luxury boutiques and fast fashion outlets.

SHANGHAI CHIC

The traditional lanes and *shikumen* houses of Xintiandi are now a hotbed of big designer brands. For funkier fashions, head over to the adjoining Xintiandi Style mall (245 Madang Road), where hip young designers from Shanghai and across Asia showcase their latest collections. IAPM Mall (999 Huaihai Road C) is one of the city's newest and swankiest malls with great dining and an IMAX cinema in the penthouse.

In the former French Concession, the narrow residential lanes of Tianzifang (Lane 210 Taikang Road) are packed with local designer boutiques, trinket stalls and alfresco cafés – it's a great place to pick up some one-off souvenirs. Look out for hand-embroidered ethnic-styled accessories at Harvest Studio (Suite 18, Bldg 3, Lane 210 Tai-

Shoppers in Xujiahui   *Passing the luxury retailer Ferragamo on Nanjing Road West*

kang Road) and photographic prints of Shanghai scenes at Deke Erh Art Centre (No. 2, Lane 210 Taikang Road).

The streets around the Bund also harbour some gems among the showier boutiques. Check out Suzhou Cobblers (Room 101, 17 Fuzhou Road) for a pair of handcrafted silk slippers, Blue China White (Room 103, 17 Fuzhou Road) offering hand-painted Jingdezhen porcelain tableware, Song Fang Maison de The (19 Fuzhou Road) for fine teas in funky tins decorated with Mao-era propaganda art and Annabel Lee Shanghai (No. 1, Lane 8 Zhongshan East Road) for its gorgeous selection of lush silk accessories.

Across the river in Pudong, the sparkling IFC Mall (8 Century Avenue) is one of the city's best, and is home to an excellent food court and supermarket in the basement. Directly opposite, Superbrand Mall (168 Lujiazui Road W) is one of Asia's largest retail complexes, featuring a staggering 13 storeys of high-street labels, plus an Egyptian-themed cineplex and an ice-skating rink.

Art and antiques
The M50 art district at 50 Moganshan Road beside Suzhou Creek is the place to pick up a piece of contemporary Chinese art from the myriad galleries and artists' workshops. Vanguard Gallery (Bldg 4; www.vanguardgallery.com), OV Gallery (Room 207; www.ovgallery.com) and ShanghART (Building 16; www.shanghartgallery.com) come recommended.

Dongtai Road Antique Market, close to the Old City, is a street market lined with outdoor hawkers selling fun repro-antique trinkets and 'Mao-morabilia' that make great souvenirs. Be prepared to haggle. For genuine Art Deco antiques, duck into the established stores set back from the street.

Shanghai is close to China's freshwater pearling areas, and you can pick up well-priced pearls, and have them strung, at Hongqiao Pearl City (3721 Hongmei Road). Porcelain and other wares can be purchased at the Shanghai Jingdezhen Porcelain Store (212 Shanxi Road N), while tea and Yixing pots are plentiful at the Shanghai Huangshan Tea Company (605 Huaihai Road C).

Custom-made clothing
Custom tailor shops abound in Shanghai. One of the best – with top-drawer prices to match – is the French Tailor (7 Dongping Road; tel: 5465 2468). Equally fine threads can be had from Dave's Custom Tailoring (No.6, Lane 288 Wuyuan Road; tel: 5404 0001).

At the cheap and cheerful end of the spectrum is the South Bund Fabric Market (399 Lujiabang Road), a three-storey warren of small stores selling bolts of material in every guise. Tailors stand ready with scissors and thread once you've made your choice and can whip up custom-fit copies of your own clothing or of one of their designs in as little as 24 hours.

Ballet at the Shanghai International Culture and Art Festival

ENTERTAINMENT

With its string of glamorous bars and world-renowned party scene, it's easy to understand why Shanghai has been dubbed 'the city that never sleeps'. There's also a calendar bursting with festivals and a fine array of art galleries.

China's most cosmopolitan city prides itself on its spectacular arts and entertainment scene. Huge investment in cultural venues in recent years means Shanghai now has several world-class theatres and concert halls, which regularly stage musicals, concerts, dance performances, Chinese opera, drama and even rock concerts throughout the year. For a detailed list of performances in Shanghai, check out www.culture.sh.cn. You can book tickets via the website hotline (6217 2426) or direct with the venue.

DANCE AND ACROBATICS

Local talent includes the excellent Shanghai Ballet and the Jin Xing Modern Dance Company. A must-see is the Shanghai Acrobatic Troupe, justly renowned for its breathtaking contortions and stunts mixed with multimedia technology – the group performs at Circus World and the Shanghai Gong Stage near the Bund.

MUSIC AND OPERA

Founded in 1952, the Shanghai Philharmonic Orchestra has since carved out a reputation for solid musicianship. For a more local flavour, check out the Shanghai Chinese Orchestra – it was China's first large-scale modern ensemble made up of traditional Chinese instruments. The centre for Chinese opera is the Yifu Theatre. Occasionally, the oldest form of Chinese opera (Kunju) is performed here too.

FILM

Despite the abundance of cheap counterfeit DVDs, cineplexes continue to be popular. Most Chinese films are shown without subtitles. Hollywood blockbusters are screened in English with Chinese subtitles at selected cinemas; otherwise they are dubbed into Chinese. China's booming film industry is currently the world's second-largest, with a huge movie-making output and new cinemas being opened across the country. Hollywood is also regularly inspired by Shanghai – several scenes from the 2012 James Bond movie *Skyfall* were shot in the city.

ART GALLERIES

The largest concentration of galleries is at M50 (No. 50 Moganshan Road).

Shanghai Peking Opera Troupe

Clustered here in old warehouses by Suzhou Creek are some of the city's most interesting art galleries showcasing cutting-edge works. Entrance to the galleries is usually free, and most are closed on Sundays or Mondays (it's best to call ahead to confirm). Two state-run modern art institutions occupy refitted structures from the 2010 Shanghai World Expo. The China Art Palace (Zone A, Pudong Rd, World Expo Park Pudong) is housed in the red crown-like former China Pavilion in Pudong, and the Power Station of Art (Lane 20, Huayuangang Rd) is located in an 1890s power plant on the opposite bank of the Huangpu River.

The city's major art festival, the Shanghai Biennale, takes place in even-numbered years at the Power Station of Art, while the privately run BolognaFiere ShContemporary, held in September, features cutting-edge Chinese contemporary art.

NIGHTLIFE

Shanghai really comes alive after dark. The more upscale bars are along the Bund, Xintiandi and dotted throughout the former French Concession and Jing'an district. Other popular bar strips can be found along Yongfu Road and Yongkang Road.

While Shanghai's live music scene is not as vibrant as Beijing's, the city does hold its own. A handful of underground clubs, including the Shelter and Yuyintang, host live rock gigs and celebrity DJs, but jazz has been king in Shanghai since the 1920s. The city has several first-rate jazz clubs that attract top musicians from China and around the world – JZ Club and House of Blues & Jazz are favourites. Drinks prices are comparable to other major world cities.

Shanghai's free listings magazines and nightlife websites provide extensive bar and nightclub listings as well as current events. The most reliable sources of information are www.smartshanghai.com and City Weekend (www.cityweekend.com.cn).

FESTIVALS

The city hosts a wide range of annual festivals, generally held during the milder months of spring and autumn. Chinese festivals such as Chinese New Year (January/February) and the Mid-Autumn Festival (September) involve fireworks, temple visits, dragon boat races and other traditional celebrations.

Government-sponsored cultural festivals, including the Shanghai International Film Festival (June), Shanghai Fashion Week (April/October) and Shanghai International Culture and Arts Festival (October/November), are steadily growing in stature. Well-run independent festivals to look out for are the Shanghai Literary Festival and JUE Music + Art (both held in March), and the biannual Eco Design Fair (April/November).

The iconic Pudong skyline

ARCHITECTURE

Mixing Art Deco, Postmodernist, Song Dynasty, Tudor, uber-modern and just plain kitsch, Shanghai is a stimulating showcase of architectural treasures that will take your breath away.

Everyone catches their breath the first time they glimpse Shanghai's skyline. The city has undergone the biggest urban building boom the world has known, and the sheer scale and speed of construction are astounding. This urban boom echoes another one a century earlier, and the juxtaposition of avant-garde glass-and-steel towers and historic brick buildings provides a wonderfully arresting sight.

CONCESSION ERA

For 40 years after the Communists' victory in 1949, construction virtually halted in Shanghai. Thus, when restrictions on development were lifted in the early 1990s, the city was a time capsule of pre-1949 architecture. While it's sad to see so many historic buildings razed to make way for highways and skyscrapers, it's important to remember that the city has always been about being modern. In the 1920s and 30s, modernity meant Art Deco. Known for its ability to weave outside ideas into local culture, Shanghai adapted the born-in-the-West style to China, and it became a symbol of the city.

Lane houses

The most typical Shanghainese architectural form is the *lilong* or *longtang* (lane) neighbourhood. First built during the Taiping Rebellion (1853–64), when affluent Chinese from nearby provinces fled to Shanghai and the safety of the Concessions, *longtangs* are a uniquely Shanghainese hybrid: based on the southern Chinese courtyard house, the buildings have multiple storeys and Western-style exterior decoration.

Lane neighbourhoods typically cover a city block, with a few entrances from the street that can be locked by iron gates. Within the neighbourhood lanes are arrayed in a matrix pattern, the stone-framed doors *(shikumen)* facing south. Because the houses are cramped, the lanes are treated as living space, where laundry is done, hair is washed and vegetables are peeled.

The concessions

No visit is complete without a stroll along the Bund, with its striking panorama of European buildings: about half of the 24 structures were built in the 1920s, and nine during the previous two decades (see page 28). Most

A detail of the 1933 Building

Traditional architectural flourishes in a shopping centre

incorporate the neoclassical themes prevalent during the period, including the regal 1923 Pudong Development Bank (built as the Hongkong and Shanghai Bank) and the Waldorf Astoria (built as the Shanghai Club). The most famous is the Art Deco Fairmont Peace Hotel (formerly the Cathay Hotel); the oldest is the former British Consulate (1874).

Old Shanghai did business in the International Settlement, but preferred to live in the tree-lined French Concession, where the Mediterranean, Tudor and Art Deco homes still stand. Many are private residences, but some are open to the public, such as the magnificent Shanghai Arts and Crafts Museum (see page 55) and the former home of the wealthy industrialist Rong family, now the Xuhui Children's Palace (see page 56).

MODERN SHANGHAI

Shanghai's most successful modern buildings include references to Chinese architecture or push the high-design envelope. The Shanghai Grand Theatre (People's Square Route) does both – it resembles a hyper-modern transparent temple to the arts, until you realise that its roof pays homage to classical Chinese upturned eaves. The Shanghai Centre's red columns supporting the entrance portico, meanwhile, are a clear reference to traditional motifs, while the 632m Shanghai Tower, the world's second tallest skyscraper, is meant to resemble the twisting tail of a mythical Chinese dragon.

Postmodern European architects have also proved popular: the seagull-inspired Pudong International Airport and the ceramic-and-glass Oriental Arts Centre were both designed by French architect Paul Andreu. An earlier and less exalted example is the space-age Pearl Oriental Tower, constructed in 1994 and said to have been built to divert attention from the Bund on the opposite riverbank – a symbol of the city's 'humiliating' colonial past. If so, the tower has proved to be a resounding success.

FUTURE SHANGHAI

The pace of change has been tremendous over the past 15 years, and shows no signs of abating. The largest redevelopment is the 74 sq km (29 sq miles) along the banks of the Huangpu River on the Puxi side, much of which will be green space. The Shiliupu Wharf has been transformed from dingy warehouses to a vibrant waterfront hub of shopping, dining and entertainment. In Hongkou, an international cruise ship terminal has opened, with luxury hotels, shopping and entertainment under way. On the Pudong side, Harbour City is gradually filling up with luxury hotels, residences and a yacht marina. Finally, a carbon-neutral satellite city is being planned for rural Chongming Island to accommodate the floods of migrants.

Shanghai traded with Britain in the 19th century

HISTORY: KEY DATES

In its transformation from fishing village to bustling trading port and now China's leading city, Shanghai has survived wars, foreign takeovers and 20th-century turmoil.

4000 BC	Prehistoric hunter-gatherers settle in the Yangtze Delta.
1000 BC	A tiny farming and fishing village is established on the banks of the Huangpu River.
AD 500–1300	Shanghai grows in size and importance, and it develops a trading culture during the Southern Song Dynasty (1127–1279).
1400s	The Huangpu is dredged several times, setting the stage for commercial success.
1554	Shanghai builds a wall to protect itself from Japanese pirates; the circular edges of the wall still define the borders of the Old Town.
1685	The Qing Dynasty opens a customs office, and Shanghai grows in commercial importance, with cotton, silk and tea the key exports.
1760	The Qianlong emperor restricts all foreign trade to Canton.
1839–45	The British Army invades China and proceeds to take China's coastal cities by force. In 1842, the Qing government is forced to sign the Treaty of Nanjing, which gives Britain a foreign concession in Shanghai.
1849	The French establish their own settlement along Huangpu River.
1851–4	The Taiping Rebellion rages across China, and Chinese residents pour into Shanghai.
1850s	Shanghai's boisterous Golden Age begins, and it becomes one of the fastest-growing and most famous cities on earth. It is rife with crime, but rich in opportunity for both Chinese and Westerners.
1864	Decisive Taiping rebellion is quelled by Qing forces.
1895	Following China's defeat in the Sino-Japanese War, the Treaty of Shimonoseki allows the Japanese to set up factories in Shanghai as well as other treaty port cities. Other foreign powers follow suit.
1911	The Qing Dynasty collapses, and a weak and fragmented Nationalist government takes over the Republic of China.

Chinese gunners in 1937   *Dressed as Liberation Army soldiers on National Day*

1921	The Chinese Communist Party is founded in Shanghai; Mao Zedong attends the meeting.
1923	The Hongkong and Shanghai Bank Building opens on the Bund.
1931–41	Shanghai becomes a safe haven for some 20,000 Jews fleeing persecution in Europe.
1931–2	Japan bombs and invades Shanghai, but withdraws under the weight of international pressure.
1937	Japan bombs and invades Shanghai again, destroying many buildings and driving scores of residents out of the city.
1949	The Communists win the Chinese Civil War and the People's Republic of China is founded.
1949–54	The government shuts down vice industries in Shanghai, including gambling dens, dance halls and brothels. In 1950, foreigners are expelled from Shanghai.
1978	Deng Xiaoping launches the 'openings and reforms' era.
1992	Deng takes his famous 'southern tour' to encourage commerce in Shanghai, which he calls the Dragon's Head of the Yangtze Delta.
1994	Former Shanghai mayor Jiang Zemin becomes president of China. Metro line 1 opens, as does the Oriental Pearl Tower in Pudong, symbol of the new city.
1998	The Jinmao Tower opens in Pudong.
1999	Pudong International Airport opens, and the city's elevated highway system is finished.
2001	Shanghai Cooperation Organisation is founded. Shanghai hosts the 9th APEC Summit.
2002	Shanghai hosts the first Tennis Masters Cup in China.
2003	Hu Jintao succeeds Jiang Zemin as president of China.
2004	Shanghai hosts the first Formula One Grand Prix in China. The high-speed Maglev rail line opens.
2008	The World Financial Centre building opens in Pudong.
2010	Shanghai holds the largest World Expo in the fair's history.
2011	The Shanghai metro becomes the longest in the world, totalling around 420km (260 miles), with more lines under construction. A high-speed rail line opens (ahead of schedule) linking Shanghai and Beijing in less than five hours.
2014	The Shanghai Tower is completed, becoming the second-tallest building in the world, at 632m (2,073ft). It forms a trio of super-skyscrapers standing side-by-side in Pudong.

BEST ROUTES

Morning exercises on the Bund

THE BUND

The Bund has been Shanghai's signature sight for over a century. This half-day stroll among its grand, early 20th-century European buildings gives a fascinating insight into the city's Concession-era past.

DISTANCE: 1.5km (1 mile)
TIME: A half-day
START: Huangpu Park
END: Gutzlaff Signal Tower
POINTS TO NOTE: To reach the starting point, take a taxi to Huangpu Park (Huangpu Gongyuan) or the metro to Nanjing East Road (Nanjing Dong Lu), then it's about a 15-minute walk. This tour can be combined with the Behind the Bund route (see page 32) for an in-depth look at the area.

Site of the first foreign settlement in Shanghai, the fabled Bund was once home to the most important banks and trading companies in the Far East. Its domes and towers formed the first glimpse of the city for arrivals in the pre-flight age, and the Bund so defined Shanghai that the People's Liberation Army marched its length when they entered the city in 1949. Even its name is a legacy of the British Empire, from the Hindi *band* (river embankment). However, it's only foreigners who call this historic strip the Bund. For generations, locals have known it as Waitan ('outer shore'); the prosaic name of the street itself is Zhongshan Dong Yi Lu (Zhongshan Road East, section one). For some Chinese, the Bund is a reminder of a shameful century of foreign domination (1843–1943), but this historic strip has now entered a new golden age as a prime dining, entertainment and shopping hub.

NORTHERN BUND

Begin at **Huangpu Park** ❶ (Huangpu Gongyuan; 500 Zhongshan No. 1 Road; daily 6am–6pm; free), at the northern end of the Bund. The former Public Garden was built on reclaimed land and opened in 1886, and was famously closed to Chinese (other than nannies of foreign children). A Socialist Realist sculpture stands on the site of the old bandstand, and next to it rises the **Monument to the People's Heroes** (Renmin Yingxiong Jinianbei) – that is, all those who fought to rid China of foreign imperialism.

The Bund at night

The 'Bund Bull' was unveiled in 2010

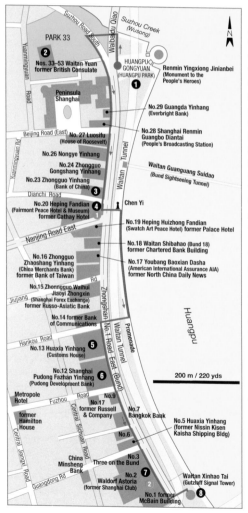

Cross at the zebra crossing at the foot of Waibaidu Bridge to see the oldest buildings on the Bund, **Nos. 33–53 Waitan Yuan ②** (daily 9am–6pm). This recently renovated pair of British Colonial beauties was built in the 1870s and served as the British Consulate and the Consul's residence until 1949. The buildings are closed to the public, but visitors can still enjoy the beautiful landscaped gardens.

Continue south past the neighbouring **Peninsula Shanghai** (Bandao Dajiudian). This newly-built Art Deco Revival hotel marks the return of the Kadoories, one of the great Sephardic Jewish families of old Shanghai, to the city where they made their fortune.

Three doors down is the **House of Roosevelt** (Luosifu) at No. 27, a grand granite-clad building built in 1922 as the Shanghai seat of Jardine Matheson & Co., the most important British trading company in the Far East. Today, it's home to several

Ornate details at the Peace Hotel

restaurants and a private club. Be sure to take in the stunning view from the eighth floor of Shanghai old and new.

Another three doors down, the 1937 **Bank of China** ❸ (Zhongguo Yinhang), at No. 23, is the only Bund building with Chinese ornamentation, the only one designed by a Chinese architect (Lu Qianshou) and one of the city's best examples of Chinese Art Deco architecture. It was from its vaults that Nationalist leader Chiang Kai-shek emptied the country's gold reserves and shipped them to Taiwan as he prepared to abandon the mainland in 1949.

The Peace Hotel

Right next door at No. 20 stands one of the legends of the Bund, the **Fairmont Peace Hotel** ❹ (Heping Fandian; www. fairmont.com), opened in 1929 as the luxurious Cathay Hotel by property tycoon Sir Victor Sassoon.

Enter on the Nanjing Road side and take the lift to the eighth floor, where some of what made the Cathay a legend remains: the vivid Art Deco ceilings and columns in the Dragon-Phoenix restaurant; the exquisite Lalique sconces lining the hallway to the magnificent ballroom. Charming **Victor's Café**, see ❶, on the ground floor, has top-notch people-watching seats by the windows.

Returning to the Bund, cross the street and pay your respects to the statue of **Chen Yi**, a Long Marcher and accomplished general who became Shanghai's first post-liberation mayor. Mount the stairs to the riverside **Bund Promenade** and gaze at the futuristic Pudong skyline. This impressive concentration of skyscrapers includes three of the 10 tallest buildings in the world: the Shanghai Tower (632m/2,073ft, second-tallest), the World Financial Centre (492m/1,614ft, fourth-tallest) and Jinmao Tower (420m/1,377ft, 12th-tallest).

SOUTHERN BUND

For a dramatic contrast, turn your attention back to the Bund, where you can see what was the tallest structure in the city in the early 20th century: the stately Edwardian red-and-white-brick **Swatch Art Peace Hotel** (Heping Huizhong Fandian), originally the Palace Hotel, at No.19. Its ornate wood-panelled and gilt-edged lobby is worth a look.

To its left stands **Bund 18** (Waitan Shibahao), winner of a UNESCO award for the exemplary restoration of the former 1927 Chartered Bank of Australia, India and China. Today it's home to Mr & Mrs Bund, named on S.Pellegrino's 'World's 50 Best Restaurants' list in 2013. The **AIA Building** (Youbang Baoxian Dasha) next door was built in 1923 and was originally the home of the *North China Daily News*.

Continue south along the promenade, heading towards the clock tower. To the tower's right at No. 14 is the 1947 former Bank of Communications building, now the Shanghai Trade Union Bank – the last edifice to be completed on the Bund

Custom House | *The Shanghai Pudong Development Bank ceiling*

before the establishment of the PRC. Its stripped Gothic Art Deco design is unique among the Neoclassical Bund buildings.

The Big Ching

Cross at the traffic lights back to the west side of the Bund and enter the **Customs House** ❺ (Laohaiguan; Mon–Fri 9am–5pm, lobby only), built in 1925. Its four-faced clock – 'Big Ching' to the British in the old days – still chimes 'the East is Red' every quarter-hour. A plaque to the right of the entrance commemorates the Communist employees of the Customs service who operated a clandestine radio here before the People's Liberation Army took the city in May 1949. Enter the lobby (during working hours) to see the lovely ceiling mosaics.

Next door at No. 12 is another Bund legend: the **Shanghai Pudong Development Bank** ❻ (Shanghai Pudong Fazhan Yinhang; Mon–Fri 9am–5pm, lobby only). When it was built in 1923 for the Hongkong and Shanghai Bank, the architect's instruction was to 'dominate the Bund'. Enter its magnificent marble lobby and admire the spectacular ceiling.

Continue south to the Bund's only Victorian edifice, **No. 6 The Bund** (Waitan Liu Hao), built in 1881. Directly next door is **No. 5 The Bund** (Waitan Wu Hao), built for the Nissin Kisen Kaisha Shipping Company in 1921.

Just a few doors down at No. 2 is perhaps the most legendary of all the Bund buildings: the former Shanghai Club, now the **Waldorf Astoria Hotel** ❼ (Shang-

hai Waitan Hua'erdaofu Jiudian; www.hilton.com). The old boys who controlled Shanghai made many business and political decisions within its burnished wood-and-leather confines. To the left as you enter the beautifully restored 1910 marble lobby (with original cage lift) is a faithful re-creation of the famous Long Bar. To the right, the **Salon de Ville**, see ❷, is a gorgeous setting for tea.

Exit and cross the Bund again to visit the 1908 **Gutzlaff Signal Tower** ❽ (Waitan Xinhao Tai, 1 Zhongshan No. 2 Road; daily 9am–11pm), which once announced weather conditions using nautical flags flown from its pinnacle.

Food and Drink

❶ VICTOR'S CAFÉ

Fairmont Peace Hotel, 20 Nanjing Road East; tel: 6321 6888; www.fairmont.com/peacehotel; $$
Victor's recreates the retro glamour of a 1930s European café, but its real draw is the freshly baked pastries and the floor-to-ceiling windows overlooking Nanjing Road.

❷ SALON DE VILLE

Waldorf Astoria Shanghai, No. 2 The Bund; tel: 6322 9988; www.waldorfastoria shanghai.com; daily 4pm–1am; $$$
Shanghai's best traditional afternoon tea, in an old-school salon complete with live classical music and windows overlooking the Bund.

Overlooking Suzhou Creek

BEHIND THE BUND

The streets behind the Bund are some of the most thrillingly atmospheric in the city, from the historic buildings and high-end dining of 'Missionary Row' to the gloriously unrestored banks and churches of the former International Settlement.

DISTANCE: 2km (1.2 miles)
TIME: A half-day
START: Peninsula Shanghai hotel
END: M Glamour Bar
POINTS TO NOTE: Take a taxi to the Peninsula Shanghai hotel to reach the starting point on Yuanmingyuan Road. Try to go on a Wednesday or Thursday to ensure access to buildings and museums that open only during business hours. This route can be combined with Route 1 (see page 28).

The area behind the Bund was once home to old Shanghai's social institutions and recreational associations such as the YWCA, the Royal Asiatic Society, the Rotary Club and the Rowing Club. Neglected for decades, they have now been given a new lease of life as part of Waitanyuan, a 'lifestyle zone' that incorporates shopping, fine dining and culture in and around the historic buildings, injecting new life into the neighbourhood.

British surveyors laid out this part of the city in a logical grid pattern. They named the streets after China's cities and provinces: cities running east to west, provinces running north to south. The pinyin system is now used to transliterate Chinese street names, but the names themselves have remained unchanged since the 19th century.

MISSIONARY ROW

From the Beijing Road entrance of the **Peninsula Shanghai** ❶ (Ban Dao Fandian; www.peninsula.com), it's just a few steps west to the foot of Yuanmingyuan Road, old Shanghai's 'Missionary Row'. Before 1949, missionaries made up a significant percentage of China's foreign population, and Shanghai was the centre of the thriving enterprise. This stretch of buildings housed the offices of many missions.

Look carefully at the carved designs around the doorframe of the **YWCA Building** ❷ (133 Yuanmingyuan Road): you can still make out the organisation's logo. The building's Chinese Art

In M Glamour Bar

Deco design was created by Chinese-American architect Poy Gum Lee, and includes an interior with bright green and red tiles with the stylised character for 'long life'. Now unoccupied, the building was once home to the Shanghai branch of the Rotary Club and *The Chinese Recorder*, a missionary journal.

A few buildings along is the **Lyceum Building** (185 Yuanmingyuan Road),

not a missionary building but a ground-breaking commercial one: built in 1937 by the Shanghai Land Investment Company.

A number of missions had their offices a few doors down at the **Missions Building** (169 Yuanmingyuan Road), including the American Bible Society, the China Council of the Presbyterian Church, the London Missionary Society, the National Bible Society of Scotland, the American Red Cross, and its main occupant, the National Christian Council.

The 'True Light' building at No. 209 is the most striking building on the street, with its dramatic Gothic Art Deco facade designed by the prolific Shanghai-based Hungarian architect László Hudec in 1933. Officially known as the **China Baptist Publication Society Building**, the group printed Baptist publications, including the *True Light* journal, Sunday school lessons and Bible tracts.

At the north end of Yuanmingyuan Road, turn right to see the latest incarnation of the **Union Church** (Suzhou

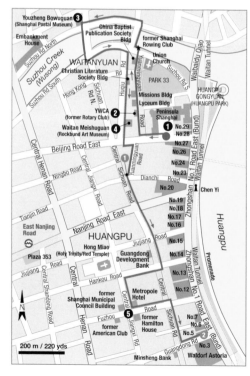

Dragon boat racing on Suzhou Creek

Road South), first established by the British on this location in 1886. Somewhat mysteriously destroyed by fire in 2007, it was reconstructed in time for the World Expo 2010 in Shanghai, but remains firmly shut, its exterior a favourite spot for brides-to-be to pose for photographs.

AROUND SUZHOU CREEK

Take a look at what remains of the Shanghai Rowing Club across Suzhou Road before turning back and crossing the Zhapu Road Bridge to the **Shanghai Postal Museum** ❸ (Shanghai Youzheng Bowuguan; 250 Suzhou Road North; Wed, Thur, Sat, Sun 9am–5pm; free). Built in 1924 to serve as the main post office for both foreigners and Chinese, the building is still a functioning post office. The Postal Museum is accessed through an entrance at the northeast corner of the second floor. The information provided on the history of the Chinese postal service is interesting enough, but the real treasure is the astounding view of Shanghai from the museum's roof terrace (open on occasion to the public).

As you stroll along the pedestrian path next to Suzhou Creek, pause and look back at Suzhou Road for a rare view of the buildings behind the Bund. It's a good vantage point to take in the **Capitol Building** (146 Huqiu Road), an Art Deco marvel of its day. The city's first air-conditioned theatre, it was constructed so that no columns obstructed the view to the movie screen.

Just west of the Postal Museum, also facing the creek, is the sinuous Art Deco facade of **Embankment House**, built in 1932 by the fabled Sir Victor Sassoon. Originally boasting 194 flats, it was Shanghai's largest apartment building at the time.

HUQIU ROAD

Cross back to Suzhou Road via the Sichuan Bridge, stopping at the midpoint for one of the city's best views, taking in Pudong, Hongkou and the buildings behind the Bund. Head east on Suzhou Road to Huqiu Road. No. 128 is the rear of the True Light building, with a different look, a different name (the **Christian Literature Society Building**) and different occupants.

Continue south on Huqiu to the **Rockbund Art Museum** ❹ (Shanghai Waitan Meishuguan; 20 Huqiu Road; Tue–Sun 10am–6pm; charge). Located in the elegant former Royal Asiatic Society building, it's another fine example of Shanghai Art Deco fusion, designed by British architect George L 'Tug' Wilson. Rotating exhibitions of modern art are spread across its four floors.

SOUTH TOWARDS FUZHOU ROAD

From here, take a detour southeast via Yuanmingyuan Road to the **Bund Tea Company**, see ❶, for tea and snacks; it's

Holy Trinity Cathedral

Elegant service at the Bund Tea Company

about two blocks south on Dianchi Road. Carry on to Central Sichuan Road and walk three blocks to the beautiful Beaux Arts Georgian **Guangdong Development Bank** (Guangdong Fazhang Yinhang) at No. 261, with its distinctive octagonal tower. The former Joint Savings Society Building, it was designed by László Hudec in 1926.

A block west stands the 1866 **Holy Trinity Cathedral** (219 Jiujiang Road), a classic Gothic Revival building built in eye-catching red brick, hence the Chinese name 'Hong Miao' (Red Temple). Next to the church is the former Cathedral School for Boys, where JG Ballard, author of *Empire of the Sun*, attended primary school.

Art Deco highlights

A block south on **Jiangxi Road**, at the intersection of **Fuzhou Road** ⑤, rises a dramatic series of buildings – three Art Deco skyscrapers and one lower building in neoclassical style. The Metropole Hotel is the almost identical twin of Hamilton House, which in the 1930s housed offices, consulates and residences. Both were owned by Sir Victor Sassoon and were designed by Palmer & Turner. The lower building is the former Shanghai Municipal Council Chambers.

A short detour west on Fuzhou Road will bring you to a lovely 1924 red-brick Federalist-style building at No. 209 – the former Shanghai American Club, now empty.

Continue south on Sichuan Road to the next corner, 93 Guangdong Road, to see one of the true 'Behind the Bund' gems: once home to the Metropolitan Life Insurance Co. Its gorgeous stained-glass windows are best viewed from the serpentine marble lobby, so do go in if the building is open.

You're only a block from the Bund, so a post-walk tipple is definitely in order – and there is no better place than **M Glamour Bar**, see ②, at 20 Guangdong Road, with its trio of bars and spectacular views.

Food and Drink

① BUND TEA COMPANY

100 Dianchi Road; tel: 6329 0989; daily 4–10pm; $
This historic British tea-trading company building houses a charming teahouse featuring an assortment of bespoke brews to taste and purchase, including green, black and flower teas.

② M GLAMOUR BAR

No. 5 The Bund (entrance at 20 Guangdong Road); tel: 6329 3751; www.m-glamour.com; daily 5pm–2am; $$
Sister to M on the Bund, M Glamour Bar has a cocktail bar, a wine bar and a champagne bar, plus a substantial food menu. The views of the Bund and the Shanghai skyline are stunning and the sophistication level is high.

Shanghai Art Museum

PEOPLE'S SQUARE

The main square contains the very best of the modern city, from cutting-edge contemporary art to the imposing edifice of City Hall, with the wonders of old Shanghai tucked in among the shadows. Spend a day exploring here and you'll get close to the soul of the city.

DISTANCE: 2.5km (1.5 miles)
TIME: A full day
START: People's Park
END: Park Hotel
POINTS TO NOTE: Take the metro to People's Square to reach the start (it's the main interchange, so you can take any number of lines) or ask a taxi to drop you at the park entrance on Nanjing Road. This museum-laden route is ideal for art- and culture-lovers, and anyone o n a rainy day.

People's Square is at the very heart of Shanghai, its exact centre and its showcase, home to world-class museums, a theatre, five-star hotels and the imposing City Hall in the middle of it all. The buildings, all raised in the late 1990s and each one a significant architectural statement, seem to have been lifted from a futuristic urban planner's utopia. They also symbolise Shanghai's arrival as a city that can compete on its own merit on the world stage.

Although there is little in People's Square itself to remind you of the past, this was the Shanghai Racecourse, so brazenly bourgeois and decadent that it had to be razed and paved over for proletarian Shanghai. Here, millionaires would ride their steeds and their wives would wager fans and sun-bonnets because betting money was considered to vulgar. The wartime Japanese used the racetrack as a holding camp and the post-war Kuomintang government turned it into a sports arena. By 1952, the new Communist government had paved over part of the racetrack and turned the rest into a park for recreation. Today, the square's buildings – each one an architectural achievement – symbolise the economic and cultural progress of modern Shanghai.

PEOPLE'S PARK

Enter **People's Park ❶** (Renmin Gongyuan; 6am–6pm; free) from the north (Nanjing Road) or east (People's Square metro station). The building of modern

T'ai chi in People's Park

Shanghai has encroached on the park, reducing its size, but it remains a lush oasis in the heart of the city with pretty tree-lined paths, a small lake and rock gardens. Come on a Sunday and you may see parents matchmaking for their adult children, clutching photos, posters and CVs in the hope of pairing them off.

Art centres

Follow the signs to the **Museum of Contemporary Art (MoCA)** ❷ (Shanghai Dangdai Yishu Guan; 231 Nanjing Road West, in People's Park; www.mocashanghai.org; daily 9am–6pm, subject to change – confirm hours for each exhibition on the website; charge). The city's first independent contemporary art museum features both international and Chinese contemporary works. Despite its relatively small size, MoCA shows some of the more cutting-edge, thought-provoking modern art in the city. Exhibitions, which change every two months, are on the first two floors of the three-storey glass structure, while a restaurant with an outdoor terrace overlooking the park is on the third.

Exit the park on Nanjing Road and head west through the imposing gates of the 1933 Shanghai Race Club building. The elegant neoclassical building with its distinctive stone clock tower once marked the racecourse's finishing straight. Look for the 'SRC' engraved over the building's entrance and the horse heads on the ironwork banisters. This was the former home of the Shanghai Art Museum until it moved to the larger Power Station of Art in 2013, and while much of the building presently stands empty, you can head past the surly guards and take the lift to **Kathleen's** 5, see ❶, page 41, on the rooftop – a good spot for lunch or a drink with great views over People's Square.

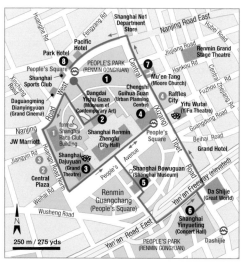

Traditional boats in Shanghai Museum

From here, walk south along Huangpi Road, passing the 60-storey Tomorrow Square tower, a space-age structure that twists on its own axis two-thirds of its way up, then slims into a hollow pinnacle that glows different colours by night. The cosy JW Marriott hotel library on the 60th floor is recognised as the world's highest by the Guinness World Records.

A little further along Huangpi Road, you can stop at **Wagas**, see ②, page 41, in Central Plaza for a sandwich or coffee, or head next door to sample the drinks on offer at chic cocktail lounge **Constellation**, see ③, page 41, if you're feeling in the mood for something a little stronger.

Continue to People's Avenue and the **Shanghai Grand Theatre** ❸ (Shanghai Dajuyuan; 300 People's Avenue; tickets tel: 6372 3833; www. shgtheatre.com; tours Mon 9–11am; charge). Designed by French architect Jean-Marie Charpentier, the futuristic glass confection is noticeable for its flamboyantly upturned eaves, mimicking a traditional Chinese roof.

Dubbed the 'Crystal Palace' by locals, the 1,800-seat theatre hosts a packed season of ballet, classical music and opera, some imported and some local. The Monday tours are a great way to get an insider's look at the theatre. Or if you can, try to catch one of the performances held here to fully appreciate the venue's excellent acoustics.

SHANGHAI URBAN PLANNING CENTRE

Continue east along People's Avenue, past Shanghai City Hall (which will almost certainly interfere with your mobile phone reception) to the **Shanghai Urban Planning Centre** ❹ (Shanghai Chengshi Guihua Guan; 100 People's Avenue; www.supec.org; Tue–Sun 9am–5pm [last entrance at 4pm]; charge, extra with audio guide) to make some sense of urban Shanghai. The museum's highlights are on the third floor: the remarkable 500 sq m (5,380 sq ft) scale model of Shanghai depicts every building over six storeys high, including ones as yet unbuilt. Also on this floor is the not-to-be-missed *Journey of Wonder in Shanghai*, a 360-degree movie that takes the audience on a bird's-eye flight across the city. For another excellent view, the top-floor café – which is almost always empty – has wonderful views across People's Square.

SHANGHAI MUSEUM

From the Urban Planning Centre, find the underground passageway that will take you to the south side of People's Avenue; this passage was actually one of numerous bomb shelters built in the 1960s in the aftermath of the Sino-Soviet split, when the country lived in fear of a Soviet invasion. From here you can follow the signs to

Shanghai Museum artefact

The bold exterior of the Urban Planning Centre

the **Shanghai Museum** ❺ (Shanghai Bowuguan; 201 People's Avenue; www. shanghaimuseum.net; daily 9am–5pm [last entry 4pm]; free, charge for Acoustiguide rental plus deposit). Cross the landscaped plaza and pass the soaring musical fountain – full of kids trying to cool off in summer – to reach the distinctive round, granite building.

This is probably the best museum in the country. Shaped like a *ding* (a traditional cooking vessel), it focuses on the arts and crafts of China in its 11 permanent galleries, arranged thematically across four floors. Be sure to visit the Ancient Bronze Gallery, the Ancient Chinese Ceramic Gallery, which traces this born-in-China craft from the Neolithic Yellow River cultures to the Qing Dynasty. Other must-sees include the nation's largest collection of Chinese paintings in the Chinese Painting Gallery and the colourful Chinese Minorities Nationalities Gallery. Allow at least a couple of hours here.

HIGHLIGHTS FROM THE GOLDEN AGE

Like a brand-new portrait set within an antique frame, the ultra-modern core of Shanghai is surrounded by the legends that defined old Shanghai: its tallest building, best theatre and wildest entertainment. Leave the museum via the south entrance and cross busy Yan'an Road to the elegant neoclassical **Shanghai Concert Hall** ❻ (Shang-hai Yinyueting). Built in 1930 as the Nanking Theatre, the building was uprooted in 2004, on the occasion of its 75th anniversary, and slowly moved 66.46 metres southeast on special rollers to make way for an extension of the Yan'an highway. The cost of shifting it out of harm's way was a cool RMB150 million. In its new position, it's today home to the Shanghai Philharmonic Orchestra.

László Hudec

László Hudec (1893–1958) was already a chartered architect when, as a lieutenant in the Austro-Hungarian army, he was taken prisoner by the Russian army and sent to a Siberian prison camp. Hudec eventually escaped and made his way to Shanghai, where he found work with the American architectural firm RA Curry. There, he designed dozens of important buildings, including the American Club and the Normandie ISS Apartments. But his real masterpieces were created after 1925, when he set up his own firm. Inspired by the modernist architecture of New York, Hudec designed some of Shanghai's most innovative buildings, three of which are within a few metres of each other along Nanjing Road and Xizang (Tibet) Road: the Art Deco Grand Theatre cinema, the Park Hotel and the Moore Church. Today, he is considered Shanghai's master architect.

'Zero Center Point' in the Park Hotel lobby

Head east to the intersection with Tibet Road, and to the wedding-cake building that dominates the corner: the legendary **Great World** (Da Shijie), controlled in the 1930s by Huang Jinrong ('Pockmarked Huang'), the head of the Concession's detective squad and a member of Shanghai's underworld Green Gang. In its heyday, the building was filled with entertainment of a mostly unsavoury nature, an endless array of smoky gambling dens, dance halls and the infamous 'staircase to nowhere' (where desperate souls could take the quick way out). Today, the Great World is locked up tight, awaiting a new lease of life.

Next door, the **Chinese YMCA** building, with its upturned eaves and ornate halls, is a beautiful example of the Sino-Western design fusion that is so distinctively Shanghai.

Walk back across Yan'an Road, pausing to admire the former **Grand Hotel** at No. 120, a grand edifice that is now a 'Worker's Cultural Palace', a legacy of the 1950s when resources formerly reserved for the moneyed classes were made available to the new masters of New China – the working classes.

If you're hungry, head to mega mall **Raffles City**, see ④, page 41, which dominates this block of Xizang (Tibet) Road and seems to be permanently packed with shoppers at any time of day. Head up to the sixth floor, where a food court offers a choice of Asian and Western delicacies.

Continue back to **Moore Church** ⑦ (Mu'en Tang; 316 Xizang Road; services Sun 7.30am, 9am, 2pm, 7pm). The 1931 church, named after the Texas Methodist who donated funds for its construction, was built by the innovative architect László Hudec and includes a surprising undulating effect in the exterior brickwork. Used as a middle school throughout the Cultural Revolution, it was the first church in Shanghai to reopen in the late 1970s, as well as the first to consecrate bishops (in 1988).

Return north then west on Nanjing Road to the line of gracious old buildings that once defined progressive Shanghai. When the eight-storey **Pacific Hotel** (Jinmen Dajiudian, 108 Nanjing Road West) was built in 1924 as the Union Insurance Building, it was the tallest building in the city, and its bell tower was used by ships for navigation.

Just west of the hotel is the **Shanghai Sports Club**, formerly the International YMCA (Chinese residents had to use the Chinese YMCA). Some of the remaining 'Old Shanghailanders' remember attending afternoon tea dances in the second-floor ballroom; local residents continued this tradition until 2010, when the ballroom was turned into an exhibition hall.

The next building down is the **Park Hotel** ⑧ (Guoji Fandian; 170 Nanjing Road West), the 24-storey Hudec masterpiece that inspired architect IM

Interior of the Grand Theatre

Pei during his 1940s childhood. Built in 1934 for the Joint Savings Society, it was Shanghai's tallest and most advanced building until the 1980s. Designed in art deco style and clad in dark Taishan brick, this pioneering deluxe hotel once featured a rooftop nightclub overlooking the Shanghai Racecourse.

Sepia-tinted photos of those halcyon days are on display, hung around the second-floor history gallery. In 1957, the rooftop flagpole was classified as Shanghai's official geographical cen-tre. Sadly, little of the original Art Deco interior survives.

Better to venture into the **Grand Cinema** 216 Nanjing Road West) next door, also Hudec's handiwork, to see its lively Art Deco lobby. Originally opened in 1933 and named the Grand Theatre, the 2,000-seat cinema was the finest of its time in China. For a glimpse of its past, the History Walk (entrance at 248 Nanjing Road West; no charge) tells the Grand's often controversial history through photos, newspaper ads and movie clips.

Food and Drink

❶ KATHLEEN'S 5

5th Floor, Shanghai Art Museum, 325 Nanjing Road West; tel: 6327 2221; www.kathleens5.com.cn; daily 10.30am–midnight; $$$

Perched atop the Shanghai Art Museum, Kathleen's 5 sits just under the old clock tower and offers spectacular views over People's Square from an outdoor terrace and glassed-in dining room. The restaurant serves continental cuisine, drinks and tea all day long.

❷ WAGAS

227 Huangpi Road (N); tel: 5375 2758; daily 7am–10pm; $$

This home-grown Shanghai brand is popular for its fresh, healthy menu of sandwiches, salads, pastas, home-made desserts and smoothies – plus free WiFi on tap. It's a good spot for a quick, tasty meal or to pick up a coffee to sip as you sightsee.

❸ CONSTELLATION

251 Huangpi Road (N); tel: 5375 2712; daily 7pm–2am; $$$

Japanese style cocktail lounge with retro Art Deco interiors and suited bartenders who concoct some of Shanghai's finest mixed drinks.

❹ RAFFLES CITY

268 Central Xizang Road; daily 10am–8pm; $

Raffles City is a Singapore brand, and its 6th-floor mega food court is a Singapore-style one, with a huge array of stalls lining the perimeter. Both Asian and Western cuisine is available here, from sushi to wontons, burgers to fresh juices.

Shoppers on pedestrianised Nanjing Road West

NANJING ROAD WEST

Nanjing Road West is well known for its luxury shopping and latte sipping opportunities, but there's much more to be discovered here: this long street is surrounded by a rich mix of religious buildings, grand mansions and neighbourhood lanes.

DISTANCE: 5km (3 miles)
TIME: A full day
START: Junction of Nanjing Road and Taixing Road
END: Hengshan Moller Villa
POINTS TO NOTE: Take the metro (line 2) to Nanjing Road West station. Avoid the weekend crowds. This walk is mostly outdoors, so save it for a dry day.

Nanjing Road's westernmost flank dominates the Jing An area. Much has changed since the time it was called Bubbling Well Road and a 1930s guidebook claimed it was 'one of the seven most interesting streets in the world'. Nowadays, the faded grandeur of its early 20th-century buildings yields to café society, where Shanghai's smart set sip lattes, before heading for the designer malls that form the bustling heart of this shopping district.

LANE LIFE

At the intersection of Nanjing Road and Taixing Road, head south on the latter and through the black ironwork gates you see ahead of you, leaving the bustle behind as you enter a **Shanghai lane neighbourhood ❶** *(lilong)*. Stroll down the lanes between the shikumen (stone gate) houses, where neighbours chat on doorsteps and children play. Return the way you came, pausing to admire the profile of the 1934 Medhurst Building on the corner of Nanjing Road and Taixing Road.

Head west along the south side of Nanjing Road, where the latest, hippest brands entice with eye-catching window displays. About a block and a half down is Meilongzhen Restaurant (Lane 22, 1081 Nanjing Road West), one of the city's most famous Shanghainese eateries. Its reputation exceeds the fare, so eat only if you're starving. However, do admire the pink-brick mansion in which it's housed (the Chinese entrance is a later addition).

Designer malls

Cross Nanjing Road to the north side, where a row of designer malls converge: Westgate Mall, CITIC Square and Plaza 66, high-ceilinged, marble-floored edifices where Shanghai's well-heeled

Elegant ties   *Shopping at the Louis Vuitton flagship*

flock to Burberry, Cartier and Louis Vuitton. Enter Jiangning Road, and next door to Westgate Mall you'll see the lovely Streamline Moderne **Majestic Theatre** with its round facade at No. 66, built in 1941 by Chinese architect Robert Fan.

Jewish legacy

Continuing north along Jiangning Road, turn left at the end of the block on to Beijing Road, then right on to Shaanxi Road North. Pass by Grace Church, built during World War II, and continue to the former **Ohel Rachel Synagogue** ❷ (Youtai Jiaotang; 500 Shaanxi Road (N); closed to public). This grand Greek Revival temple was built in 1920 by

Jacob Sassoon in memory of his wife, Rachel. The synagogue, facing Jerusalem, served as the spiritual home for the city's wealthy Sephardic Jewish community until 1952. Judaism is not one of Shanghai's five official religions (which are Taoism, Buddhism, Protestantism, Catholicism and Islam), so while the synagogue is sometimes opened up for Jewish community events, it cannot be used for religious worship.

PEI MANSION HOTEL

Lynn, see ❶, on Xikang Road, a block parallel to Shaanxi, serves excellent Shanghainese fare. After lunch here,

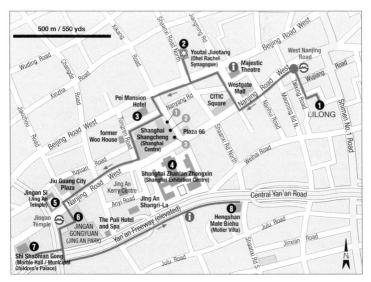

Jing An Temple

turn left on Xikang Road and then left into Nanyang Road. Past the Big Bamboo sports bar you'll find the gorgeous **Pei Mansion Hotel** ❸ (170 Nanyang Road), a Shanghai Art Deco gem built as the home of banker Pei Zuyi, whose nephew would become the renowned architect IM Pei. This is a lovely, quiet spot for a short break – take a seat in the pretty gazebo. If you have a drink at the restaurant you can explore the interior, which features a stunning staircase spiraling towards a glass dome.

SHANGHAI EXHIBITION CENTRE

Exit the Pei Mansion and head west to Tongren Road to find the former **Woo House** at No. 33. Built by László Hudec in 1938 as a private home for a dyeworks magnate, its distinctive architecture, with a round tower, is enhanced by green glazed tiles on the exterior. The interior was briefly open to the public as a restaurant, but now what was once one of the most luxurious residences in the city is closed and awaiting its next act.

Continue two blocks south on Tongren Road to its intersection with Nanjing Road West, where you'll find the landmark **Shanghai Exhibition Centre** ❹ (Shanghai Zhanlan Zhongxin; 1000 Central Yan'an Road, entrance also on Nanjing Road; daily 9am–5pm; free). The 'Russian wedding cake' was built during the 1950s as an expression of common cause between China and its long-time supporter the Soviet Union. The complex

sits on what was, until the revolution, the sprawling estate of Silas Hardoon, who arrived in Shanghai in the 1870s and died its richest resident in 1930.

Directly across the street is the John Portman & Associatesdesigned **Shanghai Centre** (Shanghai Shangcheng; 1376 Nanjing Road (W); www.shanghaicentre.com). The city's first international residential, business and hotel complex (opened in 1989) is popular with expatriates. For lunch, homegrown franchises **Element Fresh**, see ❷, and **Baker & Spice**, see ❸, are both good options. The complex also includes the Shanghai Centre Theatre, home of the renowned Shanghai Acrobatic Troupe.

Across the street, is the massive new Jing An Kerry Centre development, home to more high-end shopping, restaurants and a Shangri-La hotel.

JING AN TEMPLE AND PARK

Two blocks west is the garish, newly constructed **Jing An Temple** ❺ (Jing an Si). Now more a destination for shoppers than the devout, it was known in pre-1949 Shanghai as Bubbling Well Temple, after the effervescent well in the middle of Nanjing Road, which was removed in the 1970s. There has been a temple on this site for hundreds of years, but almost nothing from previous versions survived the 2002 construction of the present structure with its golden roofline. Especially over-the-top is the lion-topped gilded column in front of the temple,

Photo opportunity   *Exhibition Centre fountains*

which is meant to recreate a much more pleasantly proportioned column that didn't survive the Cultural Revolution.

Now cross to the south side of Nanjing Road and enter **Jing An Park ⑥** (Jingan Gongyuan; 1649 Nanjing Road (W); free). Elderly men sit on benches shaded by the enormous plane trees that lined the entrance to what was once the cemetery attached to the Bubbling Well Temple.

Leave Jing'an Park by the Huashan Road exit and head west along Yan'an Road to the **Municipal Children's Palace ⑦** (Shi Shaonian Gong; 64 Central Yan'an Road; free) where children receive instruction in the performing arts, calligraphy and (more recently) computers. Originally built in 1924 as a residence for the Kadoorie family (current owners of the Peninsula Shanghai), it was nicknamed 'Marble Hall' because of the extensive use of that stone throughout.

MOLLER VILLA

Exit on Yan'an Road and take a taxi to your final stop: a fairytale castle. At the intersection of Shaanxi Road, you'll see the steeples and spires of the **Hengshan Moller Villa ⑧** (Hengshan Male Biehu; 30 Shaanxi Road South; www.mollervilla. com), a boutique hotel named after its original owner, Swedish shipping magnate Eric Moller. Wander the grounds to get a look at the house from different perspectives, and then enter the hotel: the sheer grandeur of the place – rich wood panelling, crystal chandeliers – brings alive the glamour of old Shanghai. The story goes that a fortune teller told Hengshan Moller Villa owner Eric Moller that ill fortune would befall him if he ever finished the house, so he kept adding bits for years. When he finally finished the house in 1949, he died in a plane crash.

Food and Drink

❶ LYNN
99-1 Xikang Road; tel: 6247 0101; daily 11.30am–2pm, 6–10pm; $$
This chic restaurant serves up quality versions of Shanghainese classics in a stylish, upscale environment. The red-cooked pork and *xiaolongbao* are not to be missed.

❷ ELEMENT FRESH
Shanghai Centre, 1376 Nanjing Road (W); tel: 6385 8752; www.elementfresh.com; daily 7am–11pm; $$
This light-filled California-style eatery has terrace seating overlooking Nanjing Road. Good options include pastas, wraps, sandwiches and smoothies.

❸ BAKER & SPICE
Shanghai Centre, 1376 Nanjing Road (W); tel: 5404 2733; daily 7am–9pm; $$
A great spot for a break on Nanjing Road – both because of its outdoor terrace seating and its tempting array of freshly baked goods. The cupcakes and tarts are highly recommended.

In the Temple of the City God

THE OLD CHINESE CITY

A walk through old China – and Shanghai's 21st-century interpretation of old China – takes you past the area's ancient temples, brash bazaars and air-conditioned malls, before finding some inner peace in the classical surroundings of Yu Garden.

DISTANCE: 2km (1.2 miles)
TIME: A half-day
START: Yu Yuan metro station
END: Confucius Temple
POINTS TO NOTE: Take the metro (line 10) to Yu Yuan station and leave by Exit 1, or take a taxi to Fuyou Road/Henan Road. Go on a weekday morning to avoid the worst of the crowds – particularly at Yu Garden. It's a good route for children, but keep an eye on them among the crowds.

When the British arrived in Shanghai in 1842 they found a thriving walled city of perhaps 200,000 people, which had evolved from a small fishing settlement that had been established here for some 800 years. Earlier parts of today's 'Old City' may be a theme-park version of Ming China, but there's still some of the traditional town in the packed lanes, crowded markets and classical garden, making it a fascinating contrast to the ultra-modern glass-and-steel metropolis that surrounds it. Vast swathes of these old neighbourhoods are currently disappearing to make way for new developments – so get in quick!

FUYOU ROAD AND AROUND

Enter Fuyou Road from Henan Road. Your first hint that you're in the Old City is a ramshackle row of 19th-century shops at 384–392 Fuyou Road – look up to see the original wooden window hinges. Just ahead is the **Fuyou Road Mosque ❶** (Fuyou Lu Qingzhensi; 378 Fuyou Road; daily 6am–7pm; free), established in 1853 by Muslim traders whose ancestors had been active in Chinese commerce for a millennium. The mosque has three main halls: the original core; the main prayer hall, built in 1897; and the Art Deco-influenced entrance building, erected in 1936.

Back on Fuyou Road, head south on to Houjia Road and east on to Chen Xiangge Alley, where you'll soon spot the bright mustard walls of the **Chenxiangge Nunnery ❷** (Chenxiangge; 29 Chenxiangge Alley; daily 7am–5pm, 1st and 15th days of the lunar calen-

Lanterns at Yu Garden   *Burning incense and praying*

dar 5.30am–4pm; charge). Filial son Pan Yunduan established this temple in 1600 in honour of his mother. Briefly a factory during the Cultural Revolution, the temple was restored in 1994. A new gilded Buddha and its 384 exquisitely sculpted *luohan* (Buddhist saints) are highlights, but the real stars are the nuns, whose chanting can be heard throughout the day.

Continue down Chenxiangge Alley, turn left and then re-enter Fuyou Road, heading east (to the right). Soon you'll see the **Fuyou Road Merchandise Mart** (Fuyou Lu Shichang; daily 8am–5pm) and **Fumin Street Smallware Market** (Fumin Shang Sha; daily 8am–5pm). China is the world's factory, and pretty much *everything* can be found here at discounted prices.

TEMPLE OF THE CITY GOD

Exit the shops and head south on Anren Street. It's not uncommon to see Shanghainese out walking in these older neighbourhoods dressed in pyjamas. The lanes, and therefore the local neighbourhood, are considered to be an extension of their personal living space. At the Fangbang Road intersection, turn right and head for the **Temple of the City God** ❸ (Chenghuang Miao; 249 Central Fangbang Road; daily 8.30am–4.30pm; charge). Dedicated to the gods that protect Shanghai, this was historically the town hub. This is a post-Cultural Revolution restoration of the 1726 building, constructed in honour of the general Huo Guang. Look out for the Taoist deities wearing what look like bowler hats.

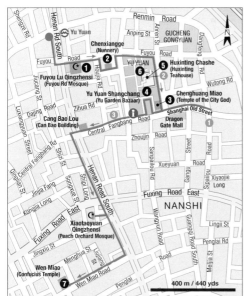

DRAGON GATE MALL

Exit the temple the way you entered, and head east (left) on Fangbang

Huxinting Teahouse

Road. **Dragon Gate Mall** on your right (168 Central Fangbang Road; daily 10am–9pm) is a sprawling vision of the 'new Old City', with H&M, Marks & Spencer and air-conditioned cafés. But we're heading for the *old* Old City. Follow Fangbang Road for about a block, where it turns into a pedestrian lane lined with 19th-century buildings. Here you'll find everything from lucky underwear shops to apothecaries, pickle specialists, rice wine purveyors, vendors with carts on the sidewalk shouting out bargains, loud music and lots of *renao* – Shanghai buzz.

For some authentic street food, turn right on to **Sipailou Road**, see ❶, marked by a *pailou* (traditional Chinese archway) and lined with the city's most delicious street food.

MING-STYLE BAZAAR

Head back to Fangbang Road and retrace your steps past the City God Temple to enter the atmospheric **Yu Garden Bazaar** ❹ (Yu Yuan Shangcheng; Central Fangbang Road, Entrance No. 6; daily 7am–late) on your right.

This bold, brash bazaar with new Ming-style buildings is a cacophony of shops, street performers, sedan-chair rides and people everywhere. Follow the signs to the **Huxinting Teahouse** ❺ (Huxinting Chashe; daily 7am–7pm), see ❷, set on a lake and accessed by the zig-zag Bridge of Nine Turnings (because evil spirits can't turn corners). The teahouse is popularly believed to be the model for

Willow Pattern plates, first created by Josiah Spode in 1790 during the heyday of the China trade and based on an original pattern called the Mandarin. The five-sided teahouse is surprisingly quiet: most people prefer to gaze from the outside. It's a rare experience to sip delicate Chinese tea from a traditional Yixing teacup on the second floor.

Yu Garden
Complete your journey across the Bridge of Nine Turnings and buy a ticket for **Yu Garden** ❻ (Yu Yuan; opposite Huxinting Teahouse; daily 8.30am–5.30pm; charge). This lovely Jiangnan-style classical garden was built in 1577 by Ming official Pan Yunduan for his father in his old age ('*yu*' means peace and comfort).

The 2-hectare (5-acre) walled garden creates a microcosm of the universe and offers ingenious views, with its 30 pavilions connected by bridges and walkways crossing fishponds and rockeries. Highlights of the garden include the Grand Rockery (Dajiashan), a 2,000-tonne, 14m (46ft) sculpture of yellow rocks; and the Exquisite Jade Rock (Yu Ling Long).

The gardens' exit brings you back to the main plaza. Near the Bridge of Nine Turnings, find the entrance to the legendary **Nanxiang Dumplings** (Nanxiang Xiaolongbao) (see page 107).

SHANGHAI OLD STREET

Leave the bazaar the way you came and continue west on Central Fang-

Prayers for good exam results

Statue at the Confucius Temple

bang Road, also known as **Shanghai Old Street**. The shops here sell Chinese-themed souvenirs: purple clay Yixing teapots, Chinese crafts, tea blends and Shanghai 'calendar girl' posters. Admire the collection of Old Shanghai memorabilia over an atmospheric cup of tea at the **Old Shanghai Teahouse** (Lao Shanghai Chaguan), see ❸.

Continue west along Shanghai Old Street and then left (south) on Henan Road. Cross over busy Fuxing East Road to reach the **Peach Orchard Mosque** (Xiaotaoyuan Qingzhensi; 52 Xiaotaoyuan Road; daily 8am–7pm; free). This working mosque, with its distinctive green domes, was built in 1917 and renovated in 1925, but its mix of Middle Eastern, Chinese and Western architecture has a surprisingly contemporary feel.

CONFUCIUS TEMPLE

Continue south on Henan Road, then right on to bustling Wen Miao Road to the **Confucius Temple** ❼ (Wen Miao; 215 Wen Miao Road; daily 9am–4.30pm; charge), where anxious students and their parents pray for good exam results by inscribing their entreaties on red paper and hanging them near the temple entrance. First established in the 18th century, the current temple dates from 1855. Of note are the God of Literature Pavilion (Kui Xing) with its Chinese arched roof, and the Respecting Classics Tower (Zunjing Ta), a collection of Chinese classics that once served as the Kuomintang

state library – and the headquarters for the Shanghai branch of the Small Swords Society during the Taiping Rebellion. A book market is held here on Sundays.

Food and Drink

❶ SIPAILOU ROAD
Off Central Fangbang East Road, between Gangu Street and Zhonghua Road; daily 8am–9pm; $
Outdoor stalls and simple cafés line this street offering everything from hand-pulled noodles and dumplings to quail-egg omelettes, kebabs, tandoor bread and fruit. Come hungry so you can try a few things.

❷ HUXINTING TEAHOUSE
Yuyuan Bazaar, opposite Yu Garden; tel: 6373 6950; daily 7am–7pm; $
A classic 'Old China' teahouse offering a variety of teas as well as snacks. Tables upstairs offer beautiful views of the treetops within Yu Garden. The tea is more expensive than elsewhere – but then again, few teahouses have this much history or atmosphere.

❸ OLD SHANGHAI TEAHOUSE
385 Central Fangbang Road; tel: 5382 1202; daily 9am–6pm; $$
This is a nostalgic slice of old Shanghai. The owner's Shanghai memorabilia is on display, and his *qipao* (cheongsam) collection is especially notable. The menu includes a wide range of teas and coffees.

Shikumen Open House Museum

XINTIANDI

A stroll through the rapidly changing neighbourhoods around Xintiandi's shopping and dining enclave takes you from the birthplace of the Chinese Communist Party to the heart of the city's consumer culture.

DISTANCE: 2km (1.2 miles)
TIME: A half-day
START: Wanshang Bird and Flower Market, Tibet Road
END: Shikumen Open House Museum
POINTS TO NOTE: Take the metro (line 10) to Laoximen station and head to the starting point. Alternatively, take a taxi to Tibet Road/Fuxing Road. This is a good route if you have children in tow.

Food and Drink

① CRYSTAL JADE

2/F, Nos. 6–7 South Block Xintiandi, Lane 123, Xingye Road; tel: 6385 8752; daily 11am–11pm; $$
Sleek decor, and top-notch dim sum and cuisine from across China. Favourites include *dan dan mian* – spicy Sichuan noodles with a chilli and peanut sauce; and *hong shao rou*, a Shanghainese pork dish. Reserve in advance.

Until recently, Xintiandi was just one of many Shanghai *lilongs*, or lane neighbourhoods. Its fortunes altered in 1999 when a developer, unable to build above the birthplace of the Communist Party next door, decided to retain the *lilong* within an upscale shopping and dining enclave. This novel gentrification project, unprecedented in China, became a nationwide sensation. Xintiandi, meaning 'new paradise', comes from a song that was popular in old Shanghai.

OLD XINTIANDI

Despite the five-star luxury being constructed all around, there are still some heritage pockets around Xintiandi, including the lane neighbourhoods, the streetside eateries and the **Wanshang Bird and Flower Market ①** (Wanshang Huaniao Shichang; 417 Tibet Road; daily 7am–7pm). During the summer cricket season, an entire section of the market is devoted to the insects, their paraphernalia and cricket fights. Songbirds are in another section, while the rest of the market is filled with more traditional pets.

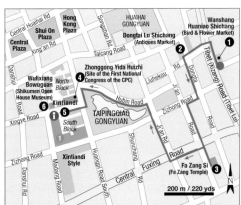

Crickets in jars for sale

Buy Mao books and jade at the Dongtai Road Market

Cross Tibet Road and walk through the archway to the **Dongtai Road Antiques Market** ❷ (Dongtai Lu Shichang; daily 10am–4pm), a mostly outdoor market covering more than two blocks, with 100 booths and two-storey shophouses with a mix of serious antiques and kitsch.

Turn left on to Dongtai Road. At the next intersection, turn right on Zizhong Road, then left on to Ji'an Road to soak up some lane neighbourhood atmosphere. On the southwest corner of Ji'an Road and Fuxing Road, you may see paper models of fully furnished houses for sale. These are burned at funerals to ensure that one's ancestors are comfortable in the afterlife.

On the east side of the street, the **Fa Zang Temple** ❸ (Fa Zang Si; 271 Ji'an Road; daily 7am–4pm; charge), built in 1932, is probably the only Chinese Buddhist temple anywhere that incorporates Western architectural elements.

NEW XINTIANDI

Return to Fuxing Road and turn left, then right on to Ji'nan Road. At Hubin Road, turn left. On your right is One Corporate Avenue, with luxury car dealerships – this was a lane neighbourhood just a decade ago.

Turn left on to Huangpi Road, then right on to Xinye Road to reach the **Site of the First National Congress of the Communist Party of China** ❹ (Zhonggong Yida Huizhi; 76 Xingye Road; daily 9am–4pm; free). It was here, at No. 106, that the Chinese Communist Party was formed in 1921. Upstairs, the history of the CCP (according to the CCP) is recounted.

From the museum exit, return to Xinye Road to the entrance to **Xintiandi** ❺, the city's most popular shopping, dining and entertainment centre in the unique setting of a re-fashioned grey-brick lane neighbourhood. On your right, the **Shikumen Open House Museum** ❻ (Wulixiang Bowuguan; Lane 181 Taicang Road, House 25; Sun–Thur 10.30am–10.30pm, Fri–Sat 11am–11pm; charge) recreates the interior of an authentic lane house. Finish with lunch at **Crystal Jade**, see ❶. Across the road, Xintiandi Style mall is filled with the boutiques of young Chinese and Asian designers.

Dancing in Fuxing Park

THE FORMER FRENCH CONCESSION

Take a walk among the parks, mansions and mysteries of the western part of the former French Concession, where many historic homes have been transformed into hip restaurants, cafés, boutiques and music venues.

> **DISTANCE:** 6km (3.7 miles)
> **TIME:** A full day
> **START:** Fuxing Park, junction of Chengdu Road and Central Fuxing Road
> **END:** French Consul's Residence, Central Huaihai Road
> **POINTS TO NOTE:** Take the metro to Xintiandi station and walk west on Fuxing Road to the starting point. Alternatively, catch a taxi to the starting point.

In old Shanghai, it was said that the British would teach you how to do business but the French would teach you how to live. It's a maxim that still holds true, as the old villas and lane houses of the former French Concession are now hubs of shopping, entertainment and dining.

FUXING PARK

Originally a military drill field and subsequently laid out in 1907 as a public park (called the 'French Park' by most locals), **Fuxing Park ❶** (Fuxing Gongyuan; junction of Central Fuxing Road and Chengdu Road; daily 6am–6pm; free) still retains its European landscaping. A well-executed statue of Karl Marx and Friedrich Engels, added in the 1990s, beams down benevolently on the carnival of Chinese martial arts, synchronised exercise and ballroom dancing that can be found here every morning. An old-school amusement park makes this a good stop for families.

Directly south of Fuxing Park, **Sinan Mansions** is a cluster of old villas that have been renovated and are now home to a collection of restaurants and shops linked by outdoor piazzas, plus an ultra-exclusive all-villa hotel.

Exit the park on to Gaolan Road and head south on Sinan Road to the **Former Residence of Sun Yat-sen ❷** (Sun Zhongshan Guju; 7 Xiangshan Road; daily 9am–4.30pm; charge), celebrated as the father of the country on both sides of the Taiwan Strait. Sun's Kuomintang Party was established in 1905 with the aim of replacing the Qing Dynasty with democratic leadership, finally succeeding in 1911. He lived here with his wife,

Okura Garden Hotel   *Fuxing Park activities include chorus singing*

Soong Ching-ling, from 1918 to 1924. Inside the well-preserved house with its plush carpets and blackwood furniture, keep an eye out for Sun's map planning the Northern Expedition and a 1924 photo of Sun and Soong beside the first aeroplane in China.

The **Former Residence of Zhou Enlai ❸** (Zhou Enlai Guju; 73 Sinan Road; daily 9.30am–4pm; charge) is further south. The much beloved Premier and Foreign Minister of the People's Republic lived here in 1946 as head of the Communist Party mission during peace talks with Chiang Kai-shek's Nationalist government. The Spanish-style villa is furnished as it was in those days; an exhibition documenting Zhou's life is displayed in a separate building.

RUIJIN GUESTHOUSE

Continue south along Sinan Road to Taikang Road and **Tianzifang**, a warren of lanes filled with galleries, boutiques, restaurants and shops. One of the best is photographer Erh Dongqiang's gallery, showcasing photographs of China's Western architecture.

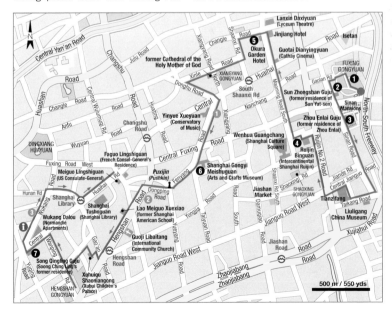

A rooster-shaped lantern at the Shanghai Arts and Crafts Museum

Exit Tianzifang at Central Jianguo Road, turn left, and then right on to Ruijin No. 2 Road. Continue past Shaoxing Road, a charming street home to a tucked-away urban park and cute cafés, Vienna Café and Old China Hand Reading Room – worth a stop if you need a reviving coffee. One block further along Ruijin No. 2 Road and you'll reach the sprawling lawns and grand manor houses of the former state-owned Ruijin Guesthouse, recently rebranded as **Intercontinental Shanghai Ruijin** ❹ (Ruijin Bingguan; 118 Ruijin No. 2 Road). HE Morriss Jr, son of the *North China Daily News* owner, built the estate with its four villas in 1928. Many buildings have been added on the grounds, but the originals remain: enter Building No. 3 to see the brilliant hues of a stained-glass window depicting a tiger in the jungle, the only surviving stained glass from the Siccawei Orphanage workshop, the rest having been lost during the Cultural Revolution. Shanghai's oldest Dao temple site, dating back 600 years, and a 14th-century water well can also be found on the pretty 100-acre grounds, surrounded by ancient cinnamon trees and wisteria vines.

Exit the guesthouse grounds on to Maoming Road, on the other side of which is the futuristic oval structure of the **Shanghai Culture Square** (Wenhua Guangchang). The underground concert hall was opened in 2011 after several years' construction.

SASSOON'S SHANGHAI

Head north on Maoming Road to the shopping hub of Central Huaihai Road. Here, amid the buzz of neon, block-long adverts and superscale shops, is a clutch of genteel old buildings, including property mogul Victor Sassoon's 1932 **Cathay Cinema** (Guotai Dianyingyuan; 870 Central Huaihai Road), an Art Deco classic that, then and now, screens Hollywood blockbusters and Chinese films.

Continue north on Maoming Road and enter the **Okura Garden Hotel** ❺ (Huayuan Fandian; 58 Maoming Road South) by the road entrance. This New Baroque beauty is the former Cercle Sportif Français – the French Club. Explore the original lobby with its glittering gold mosaics and polished marble columns, and head up the dramatic stairway. The original Grecian nudes still top the columns, and the ballroom's stunning stained-glass skylight remains intact. It is one of the earliest manifestations of Art Deco in Shanghai. The grounds are a lovely spot for a stroll.

Cross Maoming Road to the historic **Jin Jiang Hotel** (Lao Jinjiang Fandian), built by Sir Victor Sassoon in 1928 as Cathay Mansions. He soon added the Art Deco Grosvenor House (luxury apartments today) and the low-rise Grosvenor Gardens, now offices. In 1972, US President Richard Nixon and China's Foreign Minister Zhou Enlai

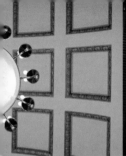

Okura Garden Hotel ceiling

Lyceum Theatre

signed the Shanghai Communiqué at the Jin Jiang, the first step towards normalising US–China relations after decades of enmity.

The **Lyceum Theatre** (Lanxin Daxiyuan) is a few steps north, at the corner of Changle Road. Built in 1930 as the home of the Shanghai Amateur Dramatic Club, legendary ballerina Margot Fonteyn performed here as a girl.

CATHEDRALS AND CONSERVATORIES

Now head west on Changle Road, turning left on Shaanxi Road and then right on Xinle Road. After a block of supremely hip fashion boutiques, you'll see the sapphire-hued onion domes of the former **Cathedral of the Holy Mother of God**. Inspired by the Cathedral of the Saviour in Moscow, this 1931 Russian Orthodox church is now an exhibition space.

Continue to Donghu Road and turn left, passing the old Donghu Hotel, a generous gift to Shanghai mafia chief Du Yuesheng in 1937 from a grateful disciple. Continue south and cross Central Huaihai Road to Fenyang Road. On your right will be the **Shanghai Conservatory of Music** (Shanghai Yinyue Xueyuan; 20 Fenyang Road; open daily), which is one of China's premier conservatories. Across Fenyang Road is chef Austin Hu's **Madison Restaurant**, see ❶, a great place to stop for lunch.

SHANGHAI ARTS AND CRAFTS MUSEUM

Proceed south on Fenyang Road, crossing Fuxing Road, and enter the **Shanghai Arts and Crafts Museum** ❻ (Shanghai Gongyi Meishuguan; 79 Fenyang Road; daily 9am–4.30pm; charge) on your left. Set in lush grounds, this grand whitewashed mansion, its curved facade reminiscent of the US White House, was designed by László Hudec in 1905 for the director of the French Compagnie des Tramways. The museum's gorgeous interior houses an eclectic collection of dying crafts including wood, ivory and jade carving, silk embroidery, needlepoint and dough modelling.

ELEGANT VILLAS

Head west on Dongping Road to **Sasha's** (Shasha), see ❷. Built in 1921 by Spanish architect Abelardo Lafuente, the mansion was the home of TV Soong, of the powerful Soong family, then said to be the richest man in the world. The villa next door was the home of TV's sister, Soong Mei-ling, wife of Nationalist China's president, Chiang Kai-shek. Adjacent to this was the home of another sister, Soong Ai-ling, married to HH Kung, head of the Bank of China. Only Soong Ching-ling, the widow of the Republic of China's first president, Sun Yat-sen, lived apart.

The Shanghai Library

From Sasha's, turn left on to Hengshan Road. A five-minute walk will take you to the ivy-covered **International Community Church** (Guojie Jiaotang; 53 Hengshan Road; English services Sun 2pm, 4pm). Founded by a group of Americans in 1925, this Gothic Revival Protestant church has hosted celebrities from US presidents to Bishop Desmond Tutu.

Continue along Hengshan Road and turn right at Gao'an Road. Enter Lane 18 to the **Xuhui Children's Palace** (Xuhuiqu Shaoniangong; 9am–4pm daily). Built in the latest Streamline Moderne style in 1939 for Rong Desheng, a member of a powerful industrialist family, the mansion is today a 'children's palace' for after-school and weekend activities.

Walk straight out of the gate down the lane and exit on to Kangping Road. Just past Wanping Road is the Shanghai headquarters of the Communist Party of China. There's no sign, but the soldiers at attention with bayoneted rifles are a sure tip-off – keep your camera in your bag.

HENGHSAN PARK AND SOONG CHING-LING'S RESIDENCE

Return to Wanping Road and head south to visit pretty **Hengshan Park** (Hengshan Gongyuan; daily 6am–6pm; free). Formerly Pétain Park, after Vichy collaborator Marshal Pétain, it was laid out by the French in 1935, and 75 years' worth of lush greenery lends it a near-tropical feel. Beginning at dawn, the park buzzes with t'ai chi practitioners, old men getting haircuts, ballroom dancers and gossiping grandmas.

Retrace your steps along Wanping Road and continue north to Huaihai Road. Head west (left) until you reach **Soong Ching-ling's Former Residence** ❼ (Song Qingling Guju; 1843 Central Huaihai Road; daily 9am–4.30pm, charge). Sun Yat-sen's young widow lived here from 1948 until she moved to Beijing in 1963, and the house stands as a monument to her and to the Communist Party to which she remained loyal despite her family's leadership roles in the opposing Kuomintang government. Visitors can see her bedroom suite, plus the living and dining rooms, with photographs of the dignitaries she entertained there, from Mao to Nehru. A modern building documents the extraordinary Soong clan in letters and artefacts, and in the garage sit two ebony limousines: a 1952 Jim, a gift from Stalin, and her own Chinese-made Red Flag.

Directly across the street are the beautiful **Normandie Apartments** (Wukang Dalou), a local landmark that dominates the north side of the street. Strongly reminiscent of Manhattan's Flatiron building, the Italianate structure was designed by László Hudec in 1924 for the Intersavin Society (ISS), and named for the great ocean liner, the Normandie, from which it gets its shape.

Sculpture on Ferguson Lane　　　　*Shanghai Arts and Crafts Museum*

AROUND WUKANG ROAD

Cross Huaihai at the 'prow' of the Normandie and head northeast on Wukang Road to the **Wukang Road Tourist Information Centre** (393 Wukang Road; daily 9am–5pm). The centre features scale models of the neighborhood's historic buildings, allowing you to see them from angles that would not otherwise be possible. About a block further, on your left, you'll find **Coffee Tree**, see ❸, among the chic cafés and restaurants of **Ferguson Lane**, a refurbished old factory.

Continue on Wukang Road and turn right on to Hunan Road, then left on to Central Huaihai Road, at the **Shan Library** (Shanghai Tushuguan; 1555 Central Huaihai Road; daily 8.30am–8.30pm). This spacious, light-filled facility, Asia's largest, houses collections of rare Chinese books, the Chinese Cultural Celebrities Manuscript Library and a genealogy section. Of particular note is a rare 8,000-volume Ming Dynasty edition of the *Taoist Scriptures*.

Exit the library and turn right on Huaihai Road. Next door, at 1517, is the Japanese Consul's residence, built for the northern warlord Duan Qi Rui around 1920. The US Consulate-General is at 1469 Huaihai Road, a neoclassical mansion built in the early part of the 20th century for prominent Chinese entrepreneur and Qing government minister Shang Shu. Across Wulumuqi Road is the French Consul General's residence, 1431 Huaihai, built in 1921 for the French Basset family. It's closed to the public, but you can spot the lovely sunflower tiles just below the eaves over the high walls.

Food and Drink

❶ MADISON RESTAURANT

No. 3 Fenyang Road, Building 2, 1F; tel: 6473 0136; daily 11am–11pm; $$
Innovative chef Austin Hu creates New American cuisine with distinctly Shanghai flavours, using locally sourced in-season ingredients from artisan and boutique producers.

❷ SASHA'S

11 Dongping Road, House No. 11; tel: 6474 6166; daily 11am–11pm; $$$
Continental cuisine in the former home of TV Soong, said to have once been the richest man in the world. The elegant second floor, with its wooden floors, high ceilings and fireplace, is the setting for Sasha's gourmet dishes.

❸ COFFEE TREE

Ferguson Lane, 376 Wukang Road; tel: 6466 0361; daily 9am–10pm; $
Casual spot with wooden floors, chalkboard specials and dishes such as lasagne, quiche and apple crumble. Lovely courtyard in good weather and very child-friendly.

League of Left Wing Writers Museum

HONGKOU JEWISH GHETTO AND LU XUN PARK

Hongkou is a thoroughly local area, almost untouched by tourism and only recently rediscovering its heritage as the locale of China's 20th-century literary uprising and as a safe haven for Jews fleeing Hitler.

DISTANCE: 5km (3 miles)
START: Hongkou Stadium metro station
END: Zhoushan Road market
POINTS TO NOTE: Take the subway to Hongkou Stadium stop or catch a taxi to Lu Xun Park to reach the starting point. The first half of this route is good for literary types, while the second half is ideal for those interested in history. There is a real dearth of decent restaurants and cafés on this route; convenience stores and street food are your best options while you're out and about.

Just across the Suzhou Creek from the Bund, 1930s Hongkou was central enough for the International Settlement to establish its support systems here – prisons, post offices, waterworks and warehouses – but far enough away for the Japanese to establish a Jewish refugee zone and for a literary revolution to ferment. This route offers a fascinating walk through fast-disappearing neighbourhoods that are laden with history.

LU XUN MEMORIALS

Lu Xun is regarded as the father of modern Chinese literature, whose insistence on using the language of the common man in literature and railing against social injustice earned him wide respect. He lived in Hongkou from 1926 until his death in 1936 and is buried in **Lu Xun Park ❶** (Luxun Gongyuan; 146 Jiangwen Road; daily 6am–6pm; free), a bustling urban park that is the centrepiece of Lu Xun territory.

Follow the signs to the tomb, where a bronze seated figure of Lu Xun welcomes visitors. His importance is signified by the inscription on his grave – penned by Mao Zedong. The trees on either side were planted by Zhou Enlai and the author's widow.

Lu Xun Memorial Hall ❷ (Lu Xun Jinianguan; daily 9am–4pm; free) is a large modern hall at the eastern end of the park whose exhibitions include a replica of his study, newspaper articles and photos from the period, as well as translations of works by and about him.

A sketch of Lu Xun   *In Lu Xun Memorial Hall*

LITERARY LEANINGS

From Lu Xun Park, it's a short walk south to the **Duolun Road Cultural Celebrities Street ❸** (Duolun Lu Wenhua Jie), a 550m (1,804ft) L-shaped pedestrian street where Lu Xun and other literary figures lived and socialised at the teahouses and bookstores. Designated a 'cultural street' by the government, the street is dotted with significant structures, interspersed with galleries, cafes, antique stores and bronze statues of famous former residents. Look out for the Great Virtue Christian Church (Hong De Tang), built in 1928 with upturned Chinese eaves and red columns; the Xi Shi Zhong Lou bell tower; and a lavish Moorish-style house at the end of Duolun Road built by Spanish architect Lafuente, which was the home of financier HH Kung.

Also on Duolun Road is the **League of Left Wing Writers Museum ❹** (Zhongguo Zuolian Jinianguan; No. 2 Lane 201 Duolun Road; daily 9.30am–4pm; free). Founded in 1930 by a group of writers, including Lu Xun, its goal was 'struggling for proletarian liberation' through writing. Located in the former Chinese Arts University where it was founded, the museum showcases the league's works and an exhibition on the lives of the martyred writers who were executed by the Kuomintang during the Communist witch hunts in 1927.

From Duolun Road, it's a short walk northeast to **Lu Xun's Former Residence ❺** (Lu Xun Guju; No. 9, Lane 132 Shanyin Road), a plain red-brick house where he lived from 1933 until his death from tuberculosis in 1936. The small, simply furnished house is left as it was when he lived here. A clock displays the exact time Lu Xun died: 5.25am, 19 October 1936.

LITTLE VIENNA

Now take a taxi to **Huoshan Park** (Huoshan Gongyuan; 118 Huoshan Road;

Map labels:

Hongkou Football Stadium

200 m / 220 yds

Hongkou Stadium

Lu Xun's Tomb

Tian'ai Road

❶

❷

LUXUN GONGYUAN (LU XUN PARK)

Lu Xun Jinianguan (Lu Xun Memorial Hall)

Sichuan Rd North

Yijiangwan Road

Baoshan Road

HONGKOU

Huangpu Road

Sichuan Road North

Tian'ai Road

Shanyin

Lu Xun Guju (Lu Xun's Former Residence)

❺

Zhongguo Zuolian Jinianguan (League of Left Wing Writers Museum)

❹

HH Kung House

Hengbang Road

Duolun Lu Wenhua Jie (Duolun Road Cultural Celebrities Street)

❸

Hong De Tang

Yulin Road

Duolun Road

Duolun Museum of Modern Art

Sichuan Road North

East Baoxing Road

N

In Lu Xun Park

daily 6am–6pm; free) to begin an exploration of the area where some 20,000 Jewish refugees were sequestered by order of the Japanese Army during World War II.

Shanghai's Jewish presence dates back to the 19th century, when Sephardic Jewish families made the city their home, followed by Ashkenazi Jews from Russia in the early 20th century. They arrived via the trans-Siberian rail line and formed a sizeable community. The last group of Jewish immigrants to arrive were German, Austrian and Polish refugees, fleeing persecution in Europe. Unfortunately, their arrival coincided with that of the Japanese. In Huoshan Park, a plaque commemorates the district as the 'designated area for stateless refugees between 1937 and 1941'. Just opposite on Huoshan Road, at No. 119 and No. 121, are the former offices of the American Jewish Joint Distribution Committee, which raised money to help relocate Jewish refugees, including the Shanghai Jews. The 'Joint' still operates today (www.jdc.org).

Much of this historic district within the Hongkou Redevelopment Zone has been destroyed, but a few throwbacks remain. One block west at 57 Huoshan Road you'll find the Art Deco Broadway Theatre, where not only movies but also Yiddish plays were presented and Jewish musicians would play at the rooftop garden. Turn back and take a left on Zhoushan Road to soak up the bustling street life in this overcrowded neighbourhood – conditions are not too different from when the Jews were crammed in with the Chinese residents so that the Japanese could keep an eye on them. This was the area dubbed 'Little Vienna', where European refugees established meagre cafés, delicatessens and grocery stores during the war.

A left on Changyang Road brings you to the former Ohel Moishe Synagogue, now the **Shanghai Jewish Refugees Museum** ❻ (Youtairen Zai Shanghai Jinianguan; 62 Changyang Road; daily 9am–5pm; charge). Founded in 1927 by mostly Russian Ashkenazi Jews, the former synagogue was renovated in 2007. The museum tells the story of the Jewish people who fled Europe to escape Nazi persecution and ended up in Shanghai. On the second floor, former residents share their Shanghai stories on video, and two exhibition halls document the story. There's also a digital database of former Jewish residents for those tracing their roots.

TILANQIAO PRISON AND XIAHAI TEMPLE

Continuing east along Changyang Road, it's just a few steps to the entrance of **Tilanqiao Prison**, on the north side of the street, first built in 1903 by the Shanghai Municipal Government and still in use today (see page 62). Do not, under any circumstances, take photos – the guards will at the very least stop you, and possibly detain you.

Historic entrance gate   *Playing Chinese chess outside a calligraphy store*

On the south side of Changyang Road, directly opposite the prison at No. 138, is the former Ward Road Heim, a shelter set up for Jewish refugees after 1939. It's now an apartment complex, but it's possible to go in and imagine the conditions of the 2,500 refugees who lived here by 1939.

From Zhoushan Road one block north, turn left (west) on Kunming Road. About halfway down the block you'll find the vibrant yellow walls and Chinese roof of **Xiahai Temple** ❼ (Xiahai Si; 73 Kunming Road; daily 7am–4pm, charge). Xiahai ('beneath the sea') is dedicated to the sea goddess, and was traditionally where fishermen would come to pray for safe returns and good catches.

Enter to see the beautiful wooden carving and statuary and experience the atmosphere of this very local temple.

Exit the temple on Kunming Road, turn right on to Tangshan Road and at the intersection with Zhoushan Road, go north on Zhoushan until you reach the lively street market. This is one of the city's last surviving street markets, with mountains of fruit, vegetables, poultry, fish and street food – a real adventure. It's crowded, so watch your belongings and keep travel companions close.

From here, retrace your steps to Huoshan Road, from where it's a short walk to the Ocean Hotel for the **Revolving 28** restaurant, see ❶.

1933

Built in 1933, the former Shanghai Abattoir, now simply called **1933** (10 Shajing Road; www.1933shanghai.com) became Asia's most prolific slaughterhouse – not to mention an era-defining example of industrial design. Behind a palatial stone façade punctured with geometrical art deco lines, squares and portholes, the impressive conical interiors feature criss-crossing sloped concrete bridges brilliantly designed for the mass transportation of cattle, capped by a central dome. After ceasing slaughter operations, it was converted into a medicine factory in 1970, then restored and reopened in 2007 as a 'cre-

On Duolun Road

ative lifestyle hub'. Although the shops and restaurants that occupy its varied spaces are a mixed bag, it's worth a visit if you're in the area to witness this fine piece of historic industrial art.

A short ride away, towards the river-front, luxury cruise ships now dock at the Shanghai Port International Terminal in Hongkou's historic dock area, which is being transformed into a high-end enclave of hotels, shops, restaurants and offices. A pretty landscaped park traces the waterfront affording lovely views and tranquil rest stops.

If hunger calls, you're within strolling distance of Hyatt on the Bund's excellent Chinese restaurant **Xindalu**, see ②, or dazzling rooftop bar, **Vue**, with a glamorous outdoor Jacuzzi and sweeping views down the river encompassing Pudong and the Bund.

Tilanqiao Prison

Tilanqiao Prison was constructed in 1903 by the Shanghai Municipal Government as the Ward Road Jail. With 3,000 cells, it was the largest prison in the Far East, earning the nickname 'Alcatraz of the Orient'. Today, it is said to be China's largest prison. Tilanqiao has six prison blocks, including one for juveniles, a hospital, workshops, an administration block, a kitchen and laundry block, and an execution chamber.

First administered by and for foreigners under the Shanghai Municipal Council, it was used by the Japanese when they occupied China, Chiang Kai-shek's Nationalist government after that, and, since 1949, the People's Republic of China. Tilanqiao has housed prisoners of war, American Navy personnel, priests, Chinese dissidents and European civilians. Despite the urban renewal all around it, Tilanqiao remains a solid presence in the area, which suggests that it will remain Shanghai's main lock-up for some time to come.

Food and Drink

① REVOLVING 28

Ocean Hotel, 1171 Dong Da Ming Road, 27/F; tel: 6545 8888; daily 11am–11pm; $$

Shanghai's first revolving restaurant is perfectly poised over the old Jewish ghetto for a great view. The Chinese menu includes specialities such as bird's nest and abalone, as well as a range of Shanghainese dishes and dim sum.

② XINDALU

Hyatt on the Bund, 199 Huangpu Road; tel: 6393 1234 ext 6318; www.shanghai.bund.hyatt.com; daily 11.30am–2:30pm, 5.30pm–10.30pm; $$$

One of Shanghai's finest Chinese restaurants, Xindalu serves regional favourites from four bustling open kitchens. Be sure to try the Peking duck and beggar's chicken, plus the excellent dim sum selection.

Waibaidu Bridge

SUZHOU CREEK

The unassuming area along Suzhou Creek is a world away from brash, flash Shanghai. The city has evolved more slowly here, with less redevelopment, and a walk here makes a refreshing change.

DISTANCE: 4km (2.5 miles)
TIME: A full day
START: Waibaidu Bridge
END: Jade Buddha Temple
POINTS TO NOTE: Take the subway to Nanjing Road station (line 10), from where it's roughly a 15-minute walk to Waibaidu Bridge at the northern end of the Bund. Alternatively, you can take a taxi and ask to be dropped off directly at Waibaidu Bridge.

Cross over Suzhou Creek the old-fashioned way, via **Waibaidu Bridge ❶** (Waibaidu Qiao, on the northern end of the Bund). Until 1856, the only way to cross Suzhou Creek was by ferry, but when the foreign residents of the International Settlement found that inconvenient, a British entrepreneur decided to build a wooden bridge, naming it Wills Bridge after himself. Chinese residents resented being charged a toll to cross Wills Bridge, while foreigners crossed free of charge. After the Shanghai Municipal Council bought out Wills in the 1870s and eliminated the toll, the Chinese began calling it the Waibaidu Bridge – the 'free bridge'. The structure we see today is its 1907 replacement, called the 'Garden Bridge' by foreign residents. From 1937 to 1941, it served as the demarcation line between Japanese-occupied Hongkou and Zhabei and the rest of the International Settlement; it was guarded by turbaned Sikh policemen of the Shanghai Municipal Police on the Bund side and Japanese soldiers on the occupied side.

China's first steel bridge had an expected lifespan of 40 years but more than a century later is still going strong. In 2009, the entire double-span bridge was floated to a downstream workshop for restoration and reinforcement. Today, Waibaidu Bridge continues to carry auto and foot traffic across Suzhou Creek and provides great views of Pudong to the east and Hongkou to the west.

HISTORIC HOTELS

Cross the bridge on the western side to arrive at the Edwardian **Astor House Hotel ❷** (Pujiang Fandian; 15 Huangpu

In the Eastlink Gallery

Road; www.pujianghotel.com). A modest three-star today, it was once one of the city's most elegant hotels. Spanish architect Abelardo Lafuente renovated the former Peacock Ballroom, with its vaulted ceiling and stately columns, and it now makes a grand setting for breakfast. The front part of the hotel dates from 1910, but earlier buildings were the sites of numerous Shanghai firsts: the first electric light, telephone, 'talking pictures' – even Shanghai's very first taxi service. According to local lore, an Astor House bellboy, rewarded for recovering a Russian guest's wallet with a third of its contents, spent a portion of the money on a car. That car became Shanghai's first taxi and spawned the Johnson fleet, today's Qiang Sheng taxi. Photographs of luminaries who once stayed here line the lobby, including the likes of Charlie Chaplin and Albert Einstein, and you can head to through the gloriously creaky antique hallways to the third floor, where a vaulted Tudor-style hall holds a mini museum of hotel artefacts and more archival images. In the former front lawn of the Astor House, by the riverside, is the eye-catching villa-style Russian Consulate, dating back to 1916.

Head across the road to the 22-storey Art Deco **Broadway Mansions** ❸

(Shanghai Dasha; 20 Suzhou Road North; www.broadwaymansions.com), one of Asia's first high-rises. Built as an apartment block in 1934 and now a hotel, it was the location of the wartime Foreign Correspondents Club, and from its offices on the top six floors members wrote about some of Shanghai's most memorable events, including watching Marshal Chen Yi and his soldiers march in to liberate Shanghai. Head up to the 18th-floor terrace for beautiful views of Suzhou Creek, the Bund and Pudong.

SHANGHAI POSTAL MUSEUM

Head west about a block to the **Shanghai Postal Museum** ❹ (Shanghai Youzheng Bowuguan; 250 Suzhou Road North; Wed, Thur, Sat, Sun 9am–5pm; free; see page 34), the old Interna-

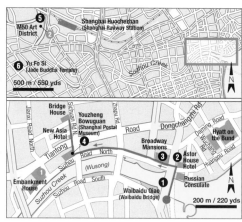

A detail of Astor House

Lighting incense at the Jade Buddha Temple

tional Settlement General Post Office and still Shanghai's main post office. The landscaped rooftop terrace (open only occasionally) affords a bird's-eye view of Suzhou Creek, Pudong, the area behind the Bund and the spreading wings of **Embankment House** (see page 34) a block west. Its 194 apartments once made it Shanghai's largest apartment block, and today several have been wonderfully restored and are available for short stays. If you're feeling hungry, the museum-like gallery of Spanish artist 'Tucho' on the ground floor hosts a tapas lounge and literary salon amidst a stunning collection of antiques and Shanghai inspired contemporary artworks, see **Chai Living Lounge**, ❶.

INTO THE M50 ART DISTRICT

Exit the museum and head north on Sichuan Road. Take in the splendid Art Deco facade of the 1934 **New Asia Hotel** (entrance at 422 Tiantong Road), en route to **Bridge House** on the next block. This unassuming apartment building was the headquarters for the Kempetai (Japanese secret police) from 1941 to 1945, and included a notorious torture chamber.

Now hail a taxi and head west to the art galleries of the **M50 Art District** ❺ (50 Moganshan Road; most galleries open daily 10am–6pm). The warehouses in this once-seedy neighbourhood on the banks of Suzhou Creek once formed the backbone of Shanghai's industry and are now the heart of Shanghai's thriving

art scene. Well-known galleries such as ShanghART (Building 16; www.shangh artgallery.com; daily 10am–6pm), which represents some of China's most sought-after artists, stand side-by-side with small boutique galleries offering an eclectic range of work. Other good ones to look out for include Italian-Chinese **Aike Gallery** (2/F, Building 1; www.dearco.it) which has a sister gal-

Modern Chinese art

China's art scene is booming, and there's no better way to experience it than with a visit to the M50 Art District. All of Shanghai's key galleries are here, covering everything from well-known artists to unknowns, and photography to installation. A stroll through the area provides a free tour of Chinese contemporary art that's better curated and more current than at any museum. With each gallery eager to educate visitors about their offerings, it's a wonderful place for aspiring art students.

Another art enclave that is emerging on the Shanghai outskirts is Shanghart Taopu (18 Wuwei Road; Tue-Wed, Fri-Sun 10am-6pm). Take a taxi from M50 to this warehouse-style art museum in a distinctive red, zig-zag building offering a bright showroom exhibiting large installation and sculpture works, a café selling art books and products, plus an original archival room. Surrounding the gallery are several artist workshops.

Monkey King performance at the Longhua Pagoda

lery in Palermo; **OV Gallery** (Room 207; www.ovgallery.com), known for its thematic exhibitions targeting contemporary social issues in China; and **Eastlink** (5/F, Building 6; www.eastlinkgallery.cn), which champions the work of China's innovative experimental artists. **Bandu Music Café**, see ②, is located close to the entrance/exit on Moganshan Road, and is a popular hangout for artists and curators on account of the cool vibe and tasty homemade dumplings.

JADE BUDDHA TEMPLE

It's a short taxi ride south of Suzhou Creek to one of Shanghai's major religious centres, **Jade Buddha Temple** ❻ (Yu Fo Si; 170 Anyuan Road; www.yufotemple. com; daily 8am–4.30pm; charge), whose brightly hued yellow temple walls stand out in an otherwise drab neighbourhood. The Song-style architecture belies the fact that this is a relatively new structure, dating from 1918. Both the temple's popularity and its name derive from its pair of exquisite jade Buddhas from Burma.

Enter the walled compound through the *san men* ('three gate') entrance. The five halls within include the Hall of Heavenly Kings, which has an enormous gilded image of the laughing Maitreya Buddha, and the Grand Hall, with the image of Sakyamuni Buddha meditating on a lotus. The temple's main draw is the pair of legendary jade Buddhas, which are housed in two separate halls. On the second floor of the Jade Buddha

Hall is the sacred Sakyamuni Buddha, which measures a vast 1.92m (6.5ft) and rests in a glass case. The creamy white, almost luminous statue of the beatifically smiling jade Buddha, draped with a gem-encrusted robe and seated in the lotus position, shows Buddha at the moment of enlightenment.

On the ground floor of the Hall of the Reclining Buddha is the other smaller, but much more exquisite reclining jade Buddha (96cm/37in), depicting a tranquil Sakyamuni with the same beatific smile at the moment of death. The larger reclining Buddha opposite is a polished stone version of the original.

Food and Drink

① CHAI LIVING LOUNGE

1/F, Embankment House, 410C Suzhou Road North; tel: 3366 3212; www.chai living.com; Tue–Sun 10am–10pm; $
Enjoy Spanish tapas and cocktails in the surroundings of Embankment House.

② BANDU MUSIC CAFÉ

1/F, Building 11, 50 Moganshan Road; tel: 6276 8267; www.bandumusic.com; Mon–Fri and Sun 10am–6.30pm, Sat 10am–10pm; $
A bohemian little café serving up a simple but eclectic menu of Chinese and Western dishes, from noodles to pizza, and good coffee. It's located next door to the Bandu Music Shop.

The reclining jade Buddha

XUJIAHUI

Sitting at the confluence of eight roads, Xujiahui is an improbable mix of brash, buzzing commerce and some of Shanghai's most revered sites. Stroll through the centuries, from Buddhist temples to electronics malls.

DISTANC: 2km (1.2 miles) plus taxis
TIME: A full day
START: Xujiahui metro station
END: Longhua Martyrs' Cemetery
POINTS TO NOTE: Take the subway to Xujiahui station and follow the exit signs to the Bibliotheca. To see the old Jesuit library, go on a Saturday and call ahead to reserve a tour.

Meaning 'Xu family village', Xujiahui is named after China's first Catholic family: Ming court official Xu Guangqi (also known as Paul Xu) was born here in 1562, and became Matteo Ricci's first noble convert and academic collaborator. Like his friend Ricci, Xu was a gifted mathematician, astronomer and linguist.

SHANGHAI LIBRARY

The local government has rebranded nine heritage sites in and around the Jesuit compound that once dominated this area as 'Xujiahui Origin'. Drop into the Tourist Centre at 166 Puxi Road next door to the Cathedral, and pick up a free ticket allowing access to each of these sites (they won't let you in without this), then follow the red-painted pathway with clear directions to the different locations.

The lovely **Shanghai Library Bibliotheca Zi-ka-wei ❶** (Shanghai Tushuguan Xujiahui Cangshu Lou; 80 Caoxi Road; tel: 6487 4095 ext. 208; Mon–Sat 9.30am–5pm; library tours Sat, but call ahead to reserve), built in 1847 on land that had been donated by Paul Xu centuries before, was Shanghai's first public library. The ground floor of the two-storey building is designed in the style of a classical Qing-era library, while the beautiful upper storey is a fine copy of the Vatican Library. The Bibliotheca holds 80,000 volumes in several languages and includes collections inherited after their owners had fled Shanghai, including that of the Royal Asiatic Society. There's a very fine wooden carving of St Ignatius of Loyola on his deathbed and another of St Francis in the public reading room on the second floor.

Right next door are the soaring twin towers and flying buttresses of the French

Shanghai Botanical Gardens

Gothic **Xujiahui Cathedral** ❷ (Xujiahui Tianzhutang; 158 Puxi Road; Mon–Sat 9–11am and 1–4pm, Sun 2–4pm; Mass (in Chinese) weekdays 7am, Sat 7am and 6pm, Sun 6am, 7.30am, 10am and 6pm). Originally called the Cathedral of St Ignatius, after the founder of the Society of Jesus order, the church has remained essentially unchanged since 1910, with the notable exception of the dramatic amputation of its 50m (165ft) twin spires and the destruction of all of its stained-glass windows during the Cultural Revolution.

The spires have been reconstructed, and new stained-glass windows created by a glass studio operated by nuns have been installed. The new panels feature

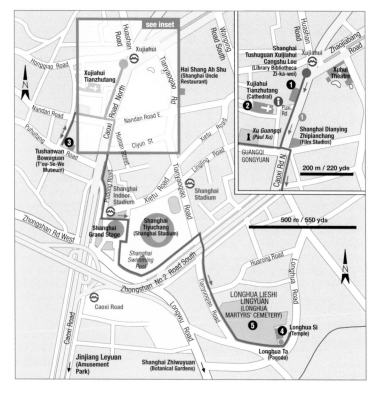

Statues at Longua Pagoda   *Shanghai Library*

Chinese images rendered as traditional papercuts, including a large rose window featuring a phoenix surrounded by the Chinese zodiac. Look high on the cathedral's exterior to see some charming gargoyles peering down.

TUSHAN WAN MUSEUM

Walk south along busy Caoxi Road for a long block, passing the statue of Paul Xu, then head west (right) on Nandan Road to **Guangqi Park** (Guangqi Gongyuan; 6am–6pm). Xu was buried here in 1641; a traditional Chinese 'spirit way' (row of ornamental columns and sculptures) was added to the tomb in 1903.

Continue west to **Tushanwan Museum** ❸ (Tushanwan Bowuguan; 55 Puihuitang Road; Tue–Sun 9am–4.30pm; free). Located in part of the old Jesuit orphanage that taught Western art and culture to its charges – and is considered the cradle of Western art in China – this excellent museum showcases the exquisite work created at the orphanage: paintings, photographs, prints and woodcarvings. The highlight is a *pailou*, or ceremonial gate, made for the Pan-Pacific Exhibition in San Francisco in 1915 and returned to Shanghai in 2010 for the World Expo.

LONGHUA PAGODA AND TEMPLE

Retrace your steps and cross Caoxi Road to the east side, to the former Zi-ka-wei Convent. After a tasteful restoration, it's now occupied by the **Ye Olde Station Restaurant**, see ❶, an excellent lunch stop. Continue north along Caoxi Road to the massive intersection, where the skyscrapers, traffic, video screens and giant adverts resemble New York's Times Square. The Grand Gateway mall here (1 Hongqiao Road) is home to several floors of shopping and a cinema.

Take a taxi southeast past Shanghai Grand Stage and the Shanghai Stadium to **Longhua Pagoda and Temple** ❹ (Longhua Ta he Si; 2853 Longhua Road; daily 7am–4.30pm; charge). The dark red wood-and-brick octagonal Longhua Pagoda looks as if it popped straight out of ancient China – which it did, since its current shape dates from an AD 922 reconstruction. The petite pagoda served as a flak tower with anti-aircraft guns during World War II and was papered over with propaganda during the Cultural Revolution.

Across a paved pedestrian street is the rambling Longhua Temple complex, Shanghai's largest and most active. Originally founded in AD 345, the Chan (Zen) Buddhist temple has been rebuilt several times and is a particularly fine example of Southern Song architecture. The current structure dates back to the 10th century.

Longhua contains some significant Buddha images: Sakyamuni Buddha's Bodhisattva form in the Hall of Heavenly Kings, and the Maitreya (or Future) Buddha incarnation, also known as the 'cloth bag monk', in the Maitreya Hall. The tem-

Shanghai Longhua Martyrs Cemetery

ple's Grand Hall features a gilded meditating Sakyamuni Buddha set under a spiralling dome, with a statue of Guanyin (the goddess of mercy) in the rear, while the Three Saints Hall showcases the three incarnations of the Buddha.

Striking Longhua's bronze bell, cast in 1894 and weighing 6,500kg (14,330lbs), exactly 108 times to erase the 108 worries of Buddhist thought has become a Shanghai New Year's Eve tradition. The Chinese New Year temple fair has also been resurrected here, with food, folk traditions and entertainment aplenty.

MARTYRS' CEMETERY

Exit the temple the way you came in and turn right on to Longhua Road to get to the **Shanghai Longhua Martyrs' Cemetery** ❺ (Longhua Lieshi Lingyuan; 180 Longhua Road; daily 9am–3.30pm; free). The cemetery commemorates the 'White Terror', the tragic massacre of young Communists by the ruling Kuomintang on 12 April 1927. In the early hours of the morning, they were roused from their beds and taken to the execution grounds at what was then the Longhua Garrison.

The cemetery today is a beautifully landscaped monument to the martyrs, with a blue-glass Louvre-esque pyramid and Memorial Hall. An eternal flame burns in front of a Herculean sculpture being swallowed by the earth, and the marble graves of the martyrs, many with heartbreakingly young photographs, lies in a semicircle. Exhibition rooms

feature re-creations of the prison. An underground passageway to the rear of the Hall leads to the eerie execution ground. Spend some time wandering the vast parklands dotted with more giant concrete socialist-realist statues and wooded groves.

SHANGHAI BOTANICAL GARDENS

If you wish to extend your sightseeing, take a taxi 2km (1.2 miles) south from Longhua Martyrs' Cemetery to the Shanghai Botanical Gardens (Shanghai Zhiwuyuan; 1100 Longwu Road; daily 8am–5pm winter, 7am–6pm summer; charge). This is a rambling expanse of lakes, pine trees and more than 9,000 plants. It's noted for its bonsai collection in the Penjing Garden, the Orchid Garden, medicinal plants and a pair of 18th-century pomegranate trees.

Food and Drink

❶ YE OLDE STATION RESTAURANT
201 Caoxi Road North; tel: 6427 2233; daily 11am–11pm; $$$
Fine Shanghainese cuisine is served up with a slice of nostalgia in this beautiful former convent. Diners can choose to be seated in the old-world dining room or in one of two restored train cars: an 1899 German model once used by the Empress Dowager or the 1919 Russian beauty that Soong Ching-ling rode around in.

Pudong's staggering skyline

PUDONG

Pudong is the face of 21st-century Shanghai, a showcase of the best, the brightest and the most advanced the city has to offer. A walk among the skyscrapers offers a peek into the China of tomorrow.

> **DISTANCE:** 2.5km (1.5 miles), plus taxis
> **TIME:** A full day
> **START:** Oriental Pearl Tower, Lujiazui Road
> **END:** Shanghai World Financial Centre, Century Boulevard
> **POINTS TO NOTE:** Take the metro to Lujiazui station, the Bund Tourist Tunnel or a taxi to the Pearl Tower. This is a great route for families.

Pudong is Future Shanghai. Anchored by the rocket-like Oriental Pearl Tower, this zone east of the Huangpu River with its forest of skyscrapers (not one was built before 1990) looks like the set of a space-age film. Much of Shanghai's fast-forward progress since 1990 has been crammed into this 350 sq km (135 sq mile) area.

SHANGHAI'S ICON

The most intriguing way to travel between the Bund and Pudong is via the Bund Sightseeing Tunnel: train cars are accompanied by flashing lights, waving 'people' on the tracks and scenes projected onto the tunnel walls. Entrance is near the Chen Yi statue on the Bund.

Begin your tour of 21st-century Shanghai with its iconic leitmotif, the **Oriental Pearl Tower** ❶ (Dongfang Mingzhu Guangbo Dianshi Ta; 2 Lujiazui Road; daily 8am–9.30pm; charge). The 468m (1,535ft) television tower – China's tallest building from 1994 to 2007, when it was usurped by the neighbouring World Financial Centre – has a series of silver- and cranberry-coloured 'pearls' along its length, three of which are open to visitors. Buy the RMB 85 ticket and zip up to the observation deck on the second accessible bauble, at 263m (862ft). The 360-degree view of the city is an excellent way to orient yourself, provided it's a clear day. A mediocre revolving restaurant serving Chinese cuisine is at 267m (876ft) and above that is the third sphere (aka the 'Space Capsule') at 350m (1,092ft), but it's almost too high for good views.

Your ticket also allows you entry into the **Shanghai Municipal History**

Cleaning the windows in full scuba gear at the Shanghai Aquarium

Museum (Shanghai Shi Lishi Bowuguan; basement of the Oriental Pearl Tower; daily 9am–9pm; charge). The two-storey museum takes you through Shanghai's history, with a Chinese perspective on the imperial invaders.

FAMILY-FRIENDLY SIGHTS

If you have kids with you, head west from the Pearl Tower on Fenghe Road to the **Shanghai Natural Wild Insect Kingdom** (Shanghai Daziran Yesheng Kunchong Guan; 1 Fenghe Road; daily 9am–5pm; charge). Scorpions and spiders are among the creepy-crawlies, and on weekends there are interactive insect shows.

From here, it's only a few steps to **Riverside Avenue** (Binjiang Dadao), a 2.5km (1.5-mile) walkway that offers great views of the Bund. Linger at the **Kitchen Salvatore Cuomo**, see ❶, for gourmet pizza.

Stroll eastwards along the promenade to the **Shanghai Ocean Aquarium** ❷ (Shanghai Haiyang Shuizuguan; 158 Yin Cheng Road North; www.sh-soa.com; daily 9am–6pm; charge), an impressive facility with a focus on Chinese sea creatures, including the endangered Yangzi alligator. The 155m (509ft) marine tunnel, with sharp-toothed sharks and giant rays swimming lazily overhead, never ceases to amaze.

JINMAO TOWER

Exit the aquarium and head southwest on Yin Cheng Road, then southwards down Century Avenue. A sky walkway allows you to avoid the wide streets as you travel between Pudong's tower blocks. Head past **Super Brand Mall** (Zhen Da Guangchang) at 168 Lujiazui Road, filled with a mix of mid-range bars, restaurants, shops and cinemas. Beyond the glittering **IFC** mall with its upscale brand names and excellent basement supermarket, enter the **Jinmao Tower** ❸ (Jin Mao Dasha; 88 Century Avenue; daily 8.30am–9.30pm; charge), designed by architect Adrian Smith, who wanted

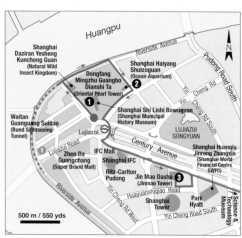

The Grand Hyatt Atrium

One of the 'pearls' on the Jinmao Tower

to evoke a pagoda with influences of Art Deco. The Grand Hyatt Shanghai's 56th-floor atrium affords a breathtaking view of the building's core, rising in a concentric spiral to the 88th floor.

SCIENCE AND TECHNOLOGY MUSEUM

From here, take a short taxi ride southeast down Century Avenue to the **Shanghai Science and Technology Museum** ❹ (Shanghai Kejiguan; 2000 Century Avenue; www.sstm.org.cn; Tue–Sun 9am–5pm; charge). The theme of the vast museum is 'man, nature, science and technology'. Five interactive halls feature everything from an exploding volcano to a mock-up of a rainforest with over 300 types of plants.

Century Park

Exit the museum and head south, across Jinxiu Road, to neighbouring **Century Park** (Shiji Gongyuan; 1001 Jinxiu Road; daily 6am–6pm), for a stroll through Pudong's green lung. Grand Theatre architect Jean-Marie Charpentier designed this 140-hectare (350-acre) eco-park, which is anchored by a huge lake.

ORIENTAL ARTS CENTRE

Exit the park on Jinxiu Road and follow the signs northwest to the adjacent **Oriental Arts Centre** (Shanghai Dongfang Yishu Zhongxin; 425 Dingxiang Road; www.shoac.com.cn). Pudong's answer to the Grand Theatre has three theatres and an exhibition hall. Viewed from above, the 23,000 sq m (247,572 sq ft) building is

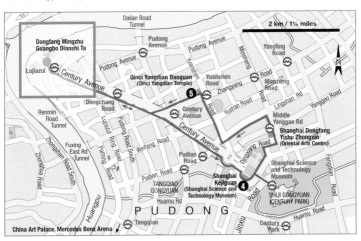

Century Boulevard and Park

in the shape of a magnolia, Shanghai's city flower.

QINCI YANGDIAN TEMPLE

Hail a taxi on Yanggao Road to the **Qinci Yangdian Temple** ❺ (Qinci Yangdian Daoguan; 476 Yuanshen Road; daily 8am–4pm; charge). The traditional Chinese roof and ochre walls of Pudong's most important temple look out of place in the midst of all this modernity. The temple was first built during the Three Kingdoms period (AD 220–80) and its most powerful deity is Yan Wang, the god of hell.

CHINA ART PALACE

The striking red **China Art Palace** (Zhonghua Yishu Gong; World Expo Park, 161 Shangnan Road; Tue–Sun 9am–5pm; free) charts the development of modern art in China, from the Qing Dynasty to today. Its large-format artworks housed in cavernous galleries are almost as impressive as the building itself – which was the China Pavilion of the 2010 World Expo, and resembles a huge red-lacquered crown made of interlocking pieces.

Nearby, another World Expo legacy icon is the oyster-shell shaped **Mercedes-Benz Arena** (1200 Expo Avenue; tel: 400 181 6688; www.mercedes-benzarena.com). The six-level, 18,000-seat arena hosts concerts by Chinese and international popstars, large-scale shows and sporting events. It also boasts Shanghai's largest ice rink, a cinema and nightclub.

SHANGHAI WORLD FINANCIAL CENTRE

From here, head back to Century Avenue to the **Shanghai World Financial Centre** (Shanghai Huanqiu Jinrong Zhongxin; 100 Century Avenue; observatory daily 8am–11pm, last ticket 10pm; charge), currently the world's fourth-tallest building at 492m (1,614ft). Enter on the western side and go to Basement 1 to purchase tickets to the observatory. SWFC's distinctive design features a trapezoidal opening at the apex, which has given the building its local nickname, 'the bottle opener'. There are sightseeing platforms on the 94th, 97th and 100th floors, with the latter's transparent floor offering the surreal experience of walking above the Pearl Tower. Finish up with dinner at Park Hyatt's 91st-floor restaurant (see page 112).

Food and Drink

❶ KITCHEN SALVATORE CUOMO

2967 Riverside Avenue; tel: 5054 1265; www.ystable.com; daily 11am–2.30pm, 6–10pm; $$$$

Fine dining with a spectacular view: chef Salvatore Cuomo is known for his gourmet pizzas and a classic Italian menu, but what sets this restaurant apart is its setting in the shadow of the Oriental Pearl Tower. Floor-to-ceiling glass walls give every seat in the house a spectacular view.

A Shaolin Kung Fu performance

SHANGHAI AFTER DARK

Experience Shanghai in all its nocturnal glory as it revels in its reputation as 'the city that never sleeps' – start with a night at the theatre and end with a Bund bar crawl.

DISTANCE: 2km (1.2 miles)
TIME: A full evening
START: Grand Theatre
END: M1NT
POINTS TO NOTE: Take the metro to People's Square station or catch a taxi to the Grand Theatre to begin.

Shanghai is well on the way to becoming a world cultural centre, with music, drama, dance and cinema all experiencing a golden age. Coupled with fantastic nightlife and a vast supply of restaurants, the options for a night on the town are almost endless.

SHANGHAI GRAND

Begin your night at the dramatic **Shanghai Grand Theatre** ❶ (Shanghai Dajuyuan; 300 People's Avenue; tickets: 6372 3833; www.shgtheatre.com). This modern 1,800-seat theatre features a wide variety of shows. Big names such as Tan Dun perform here, as do local drama groups, symphony orchestras, Chinese opera and dance troupes. Try to catch a performance of the Shanghai Ballet's Revolution-era *White-Haired Girl*, which celebrates its 50th anniversary in 2014.

YIFU THEATRE

East from the Grand Theatre is the **Yifu Theatre** ❷

Peking opera at the Yifi Theatre

(Yifu Wutai; 701 Fuzhou Road; tel: 6360 3195). Originally (and officially) known as the Tianchan Theatre, this is Shanghai's oldest Chinese opera house. Once hailed as the largest theatre in the Far East, it has featured Peking opera performances since its establishment in 1925. A new 1,000-seat, two-storey theatre with modern facilities was added in 1994. Located just across from Raffles City shopping centre, the theatre hosts troupes from around the country, but the highlight is its own Shanghai Peking opera troupe.

Peking Opera

There are more than 360 different varieties of Chinese opera, including a popular regional version (Kunju), but Peking opera remains the best-known style. It's recognisable by its falsetto singing, vivid make-up, percussion-based music, striking acrobatics and librettos based on the exploits of legendary heroes. Peking opera was king in old Shanghai; it is a highly demanding art: actors, who begin training as children, must learn not only to sing and dance, but also to acquire an extensive repertoire of highly stylised gestures and acrobatics. Few props are used, which means the audience must use their imagination to fill in the considerable blanks.

GREAT WORLD ENTERTAINMENT CENTRE

Head south along Tibet Road, crossing under the Yan'an Road Elevated Free-

way. On your left is the infamous **Great World Entertainment Centre ❸** (Da Shijie), associated in the 1930s with all of the vices that earned Shanghai its moniker as the 'Whore of the Orient'. Built in 1918 as a vaudeville-style multiplex with shows appealing to all ages, it was gradually taken over by the Shanghai underworld and filled with bars, opium dens and lewd floor shows.

After drugs, gambling and prostitution were virtually eliminated by the new regime in the 1950s, the Great World returned to the more wholesome fare of dramatic performances, concerts and children's shows. It has been unused for the past decade, but the municipal government has announced that the building, which was renovated before the 2010 World Expo, will be reopened.

SHANGHAI CONCERT HALL

Across Tibet Road from the Great World is the **Shanghai Concert Hall ❹** (Shanghai Yinyueting). Originally the Nanking Theatre, it was one of the city's popular movie theatres during the 1930s and 1940s. Today it's the venue for a wide variety of musical performances, including classical, jazz and Chinese concerts. The Shanghai Symphony Orchestra (SSO) performs its chamber music series here – try to catch a performance if you can.

Founded in 1879, the SSO began as the International Settlement's town band, evolving into a symphony first with only foreign musicians and later

In the bar at M Glamour   *Shanghai has buzzing nightlife*

with Chinese musicians, leading to the establishment of the Shanghai Conservatory in 1927. It was the graduates of this conservatory that were instrumental in persuading the Communist Party that classical music could 'serve the people', and continued to develop Western music in the post-1949 era.

BUND AREA BAR CRAWL

Begin your evening at **M Glamour**, see ➊, sister venue to the renowned M on the Bund restaurant, and quite possibly Shanghai's prettiest bar. Glamour's location at the top of the Bund makes it an ideal place to begin a bar crawl.

Directly across Guangdong Road at Three on the Bund, **Unico** (2/F, Three on the Bund; www.unico.cn.com; daily 6pm-2am, later at weekends) is a sexy Latin lounge with an impressive tapas and cocktail menu paired according to compass coordinates that span Latin America, and a regular roster of live musicians and top-name DJs that keep the dance floor swaying until late.

From Guangdong Road, walk north on the Bund to No. 18 and take the lift up to **Bar Rouge** (7/F, Bund 18, Zhongshan No. 1 Road East; www.bar-rouge-shanghai.com; Sun–Thur 6pm–1.30am, Fri–Sat 6pm–4.30am), a favourite party spot with the jet-set crowd. The bar, decorated with lipstick-red glass chandeliers, opens out on to a spectacular terrace overlooking the Pudong skyline. DJs keep the party going until the early hours.

Leave Bar Rouge and head south on the Bund. Just one block west on Fuzhou Road is the **House of Blues and Jazz** (60 Fuzhou Road; www.houseofblues andjazz.com; Tue–Sun 7pm–2am, concerts 9.30pm–1am), owned by Shanghai celebrity Dong Fu Lin. It's his passion for jazz and blues that drives the club, which is one of Shanghai's best live music venues. Late evening is the time to go, when the crowd and the music creates a real buzz. The interior feels like an old Shanghai speakeasy, with vintage items from the owner's collection.

Want to keep the party going? Head west on Fuzhou Road to **M1NT** (24/F, 318 Fuzhou Road; www.m1ntglobal.com/club-shanghai). Perhaps Shanghai's top club, the fashionable M1NT attracts top international DJs, visiting stars and local celebs. The club's dramatic entrance features a 17m (56ft) long shark tank, with over 20 white-tipped reef sharks. With its breathtaking, 360-degree views of Shanghai's glittering skyline, you may just want to stay until dawn…

Food and Drink

➊ M GLAMOUR

No. 5 The Bund (entrance at 20 Guangdong Road); tel: 6350 9988; www.m-restaurant group.com; daily 5pm–late; $$$
The cocktails are creative and the excellent food comes courtesy of M on the Bund chefs at this swanky bar-restaurant.

One of Tongli's picturesque waterways

TONGLI

The picturesque water town of Tongli, with its ancient architecture and arched bridges crisscrossing the canals, offers a glimpse of what this region looked like back in the days of the Song Dynasty.

DISTANCE: 8km (5 miles)
TIME: A full day
START: Ming Qing Jie
END: Luoxing Islet
POINTS TO NOTE: Like all of the water villages around Shanghai, Tongli is quite touristy, so try to visit on a weekday and arrive early in the morning or in the late afternoon when the tour groups have left. To get there from Shanghai, the easiest way is to hire a car for the day. There are also tour buses that depart from the Shanghai Tour Bus Centre (2409 Zhongshan No. 2 Road; tel: 2409 5555, ask for English language service). Bus tickets generally include entrance. Tongli itself is entirely navigable on foot. An entrance ticket (RMB 100) is required to enter the village, and includes free entry to three sites. Book an English-speaking guide in advance via the Tongli Tourist Information Centre (512 6333 1145). Most information in Tongli is in Chinese only, so a guide will give some useful insight into what you're looking at.

Escape from Shanghai for a day to the beguiling old water town of **Tongli**, so pretty that it's often used as a backdrop for Chinese films and television shows. Situated on the Grand Canal and surrounded by five streams, the built-up area is made up of seven islets, connected by a series of 49 ancient arched stone bridges with typically evocative names such as 'Lasting Celebration' and 'Peace and Tranquillity'. This was once a wealthy place, where retired officials and native sons who had made their fortune returned to build the finely crafted grand mansions and classical gardens that make Tongli such a treasure today.

MING QING STREET

Enter Tongli (entrance ticket required) on **Ming Qing Jie**, named for the Ming- and Qing-era wooden houses that line it. Today, the houses are filled with souvenir shops, restaurants and snack stalls. Be sure to try the local sweet lotus root *(tongli lianou)* and sweetbread called *jiu niang bing* – decent, reasonably priced

A relaxing change from big city life

versions are available at Lin's Store and Gu Xian Cun on Ming Qing Jie. You'll want to come back here for lunch at **Xiangge Jiulou**, see ❶, to try the local specialities, or the **Nanyuan Teahouse**, see ❷, for an atmospheric and quintessential experience of Tongli.

GENGLE HALL

Head west on Xinzhen Jie, admiring the ancient architecture and town's signature bridges as you go. Two blocks in, on an islet, is **Gengle Hall ❶** (Gengle Tang), evidence of the wealth that once flourished here. Ming Dynasty official Zhuxiang – who was also known as Gengle – built this mansion retreat when he retired from government service. According to local lore, he was so pleased with the result that he rarely left the 54 rooms and lovely gardens, becoming something of a hermit. Today, you can walk through

the three courtyards and some of the 41 remaining rooms, but the real star here is the garden: a zigzag bridge leads to a lovely pavilion, and outside the Sweet Osmanthus Hall the scent of the ancient sweet osmanthus trees still drifts by. Buildings are arranged around a pretty lotus pond, sited so that each has its own special view of the garden: there's a library, an art studio and a dining room.

THREE BRIDGES

Head north a block, then east at the first right turn, to a trio of bridges: **Peace Bridge** (Taiping Qiao), **Luck Bridge** (Jili Qiao) and **Lasting Celebration Bridge** (Changqing Qiao). These Ming and Qing Dynasty 'ternate' (meaning arranged in threes) bridges cross at the confluence of three rivers, creating a sort of ancient elevated highway over the water. In ancient times, it was believed that crossing the three bridges would bring good fortune on milestone occasions such as weddings and birthdays. Thus brides used to be carried across the bridges in their nuptial sedan chairs on their wedding day – and today, tourists recreate that same journey, dressed in Chinese wedding garb, to the accom-

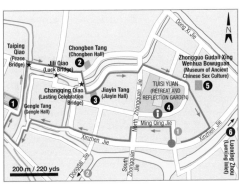

Tongli is peaceful in the morning

paniment of traditional Chinese music. Look for the couplets on Luck Bridge extolling the views.

The ternate bridges link to two mansions, **Chongben Hall** ❷ (Chongben Tang) and **Jiayin Hall** (Jiayin Tang) ❸. Tongli native son Qian Youqin built Chongben Hall, a grand two-storey house, in 1912, renovating an older residence on the property. The pretty house is smaller than Tongli's other mansions, but still has four courtyards. The highlight is its more than 100 carvings featuring symbols of good fortune, such as bats, cranes and vases, and scenes from the Chinese literary classics.

Head south across Lasting Celebration Bridge to **Jiayin Hall**, with its whitewashed walls and doorways topped with little upturned eaves. Liu Bingnan moved to Tongli and built this stunning mansion in 1922, at the then unheard-of cost of 22,000 silver taels. Jiayin's main building is designed in the Ming style, and is particularly well known for its carvings of scenes from the Chinese classical novel *The Romance of the Three Kingdoms*.

A GARDEN FOR REFLECTION

For one of the loveliest gardens anywhere, head east for about a block and a half from Jiayin Hall to the **Retreat and Reflection Garden** ❹ (Tuisi Yuan), a World Heritage site. Imperial court official Ren Lansheng created the garden in 1886, naming it after a

favourite saying of Chinese officials: 'When in office, one should be loyal to the Emperor; when away from office, one should meditate on his faults'. The 6,600-sq m (71,000-sq ft) garden is indeed a calming retreat, dotted with ponds filled with carp, ancient, shady trees, bonsais and flowering plants. The family home is in the western part of the garden, the living rooms in the centre, and a scenic garden with pavilions, walkways and rock gardens in the east.

AN UNUSUAL MUSEUM

A short walk directly east of the Garden is the **Museum of Ancient Chinese Sex Culture** ❺ (Zhongguo Gudai Xing Wenhua Bowuguan; www.china sexmuseum.com; daily 8am–5pm; charge), which was relocated here from Shanghai in 2004 because of rising rents in the city. The museum houses the private collection of noted sexologist and Shanghai University professor Liu Danyin, who has amassed a comprehensive collection of more than 1,200 artefacts on the history of Chinese sexuality. The well-curated museum is organised by themes such as sex in literature and the arts, and sex and evolution. There is insight into Chinese culture, with exhibits on foot binding, dowry trunks (explicit paintings of copulating couples at the bottom of these trunks were meant as an instruction manual

Chinese musicians in a teahouse

for newly-wed daughters), lovemaking chairs, statues and sculpture. Much of the exhibition is quite graphic.

For a different perspective on Tongli, head for the Gondolier Pier, a short walk south of the museum. You can hire a gondola (RMB 70) for a relaxing ride through the canals, sometimes accompanied by a singing gondolier.

You can also visit **Luoxing Islet** ⑥ (Luoxing Zhou), in Tongli Lake, to the east of the town – the price is included in your ticket. A pleasant boat ride takes you over to the islet, which has a strong religious legacy that dates back to the Yuan Dynasty. There are three temples here – Buddhist, Taoist and Confucian, all of which have been rebuilt in recent years.

ANCIENT WATERTOWNS

Tongli is one of several historic watertowns close to Shanghai, with ancient whitewashed houses and temples built along winding canals crisscrossed by arched stone bridges. Each of the following watertowns can be reached in a daytrip from Shanghai. Avoid weekends and public holidays when tourist crowds are out in full force.

About 90 minutes from Shanghai, **Zhouzhuang** is one of China's oldest watertowns and one of the larger ones – it's also one of the busiest. The 900-year-old Taoist Chengxu Temple provides a welcome retreat from the crowds. Pretty **Xitang** had a star-

ring role in *Mission Impossible III*, with Tom Cruise leaping across its ancient bridges. It's about an hour and a half from Shanghai and several canal-side guesthouses are available if you wish to stay the night, when the town becomes quieter and more alluring. What **Qibao** lacks in size and authenticity, it makes up for in convenience – you can reach it via Shanghai's Line 9 metro in under 30 minutes. There is a pleasant temple and a tiny shadow puppet theatre that are worth visiting.

① XIANGGE JIULOU

Ming Qing Jie; tel: 512 6333 6988; daily 8.30am–8pm; $

Serves up tasty local treats, much like the many other restaurants you'll find on Ming Qing Street, but the menu is in English. The dishes come from local Jiangsu cuisine, with an emphasis on seafood. Local specialities include smoked fish, braised pig's trotters, spring rolls and dried tofu (beancurd).

② NANYUAN TEAHOUSE

Dongkang Lu and Nankang Lu; daily 8.30am–6pm

Traditional teahouse in a restored wooden Qing-era building serves refreshments and local snacks, and offers excellent canal views from its second-storey windows. Get there early for the atmosphere: locals gather first thing in the morning to sip tea and exchange gossip.

In the Master of Nets Garden

SUZHOU

Suzhou's intricate mosaic of canals and classical gardens is as impressive today as it was when Marco Polo first visited and dubbed this ancient city the 'Venice of the East'.

DISTANCE: 6km (3.7 miles), plus taxis
TIME: A full day
START: Pan Pacific Suzhou
END: Suzhou Silk Museum
POINTS TO NOTE: The easiest and most efficient way to get to Suzhou is on the high-speed train from Shanghai, which takes just 30 minutes. The genius of Suzhou's classical gardens is that every season reveals something different. Avoid the crowds and come during winter, when the gardens take on a stark beauty.

The ancient city of Suzhou, founded in 600 BC, flourished with the completion of the Grand Canal and neighbouring Hangzhou's emergence as the imperial capital. Silk production thrived, and imperial officials laid out classical gardens – almost 200 during Suzhou's peak. The 70 remaining gardens are now a World Heritage site and form the soul of the city – each has its own distinct personality and offers a microcosm of the world, perfectly balanced in terms of harmony, proportion and variety.

Take an early train from Shanghai and then a taxi to the **Pan Pacific Suzhou**, see ❶, for breakfast (Suzhou Wugong Zhi Taipingyang Jiudian); tuck into the impressive buffet spread overlooking classical gardens and the evocative Ruigang Pagoda.

CITY SIGHTS

Head west from the Pan Pacific entrance, then south at the Dong Dajie intersection to reach the **Gusu Garden ❶** (Gusu Yuan; 1 Dong Dajie; 7.30am–5pm; charge). Stroll through the landscaped grounds and follow the signs to the **Five Gate Bridge** (Wumen Qiao), Suzhou's tallest bridge, for the age-old view of boats and barges on the canal. Directly across the main road is the **Ruigang Pagoda** (Ruigang Ta), a seven-storey, 37m (121ft) octagonal brick-and-timber pagoda that was first built in AD 1004. **Pan Gate** (Panmen), the only remaining stretch of Suzhou's third-century city wall, is a short walk southwest. Climb up the 300m (980ft) of original city wall for a view of the arched bridges below.

Chinese traditional river street in Suzhou

A CLASSICAL GARDEN

Take a taxi northeast to **Master of the Nets Garden** ❷ (Wangshi Yuan; daily 7.30am–5.30pm (winter), 7.30am–10pm (summer); charge, evening performances additional fee). The name refers to the ambition of its retired court official owner, who longed to be a fisherman. The intimate garden's charm comes from its delicate, scaled-down courtyards, pavilions and rockeries. Some of Suzhou's most exquisite antique furniture is here, notably in the Peony Study, which has been replicated at New York's Metropolitan Museum of Art. From mid-March to mid-November, the garden is the setting for traditional performances of opera, music and dance. If you're there on a moonlit night, don't miss the Moon Watching Pavilion, where you can see the moon thrice over: in the sky, in the pond and in a mirror.

NORTH TO PINGJIANG LU

From Master of the Nets, walk north along Fenghuang Jie, turn right on Ganjiang Dong Lu – passing the twin pagodas of Shuang Ta – to reach **Pingjiang Lu**, a lovely historic cobbled stretch along a willow-lined canal. The traditional buildings lining the street now house a range of shops, cafés, hotels and restaurants.

Follow the signs to the **Pingtan Museum** (Pingtan Bowuguan; daily 8.30am–noon, 1.30–3.30pm; free), just east off Pingjiang Lu, where Suzhou's ancient art of

A cannon used by Taiping Tianguo rebels, Suzhou Museum

oral storytelling comes alive. Performances are accompanied by Chinese instruments – you don't need to understand the narrative to enjoy its beauty.

Directly next door is the **Kunqu Opera Museum** (Kunqu Bowuguan; 14 Zhongzhang Jia Xiang; daily 8.30am–4.30pm; free), which chronicles the 600-year-old Chinese opera tradition from the town of Kunshan, near Suzhou. Kunqu opera is still performed here, in a Ming Dynasty building with a stunning wooden dome. Across the courtyard, a modern building serves as a second stage and houses a display of costumes, masks, musical instruments and an exhibition on the opera's history and key characters.

Head west two blocks, crossing Lindun Lu, to Guanqian Jie, another historic street, for lunch at Suzhou's famous **Song He Lou**, see ❷, renowned for its local delicacies.

HUMBLE ADMINISTRATOR'S GARDEN

After lunch, walk north on Pishi Jie then east on Xibei Jie and Dongbei Jie to reach the **Humble Administrator's Garden** ❸ (Zhuozheng Yuan; 178 Dongbei Jie; daily 7.30am–5pm, 7.30am–5.30pm Mar–mid-Nov; charge, ticket includes entry to the Garden Museum). The garden is Suzhou's largest, and its name comes from a Jin Dynasty poem: 'Cultivating a garden is the work of a humble man'. But this 4-hectare (10-acre) garden is far from a humble undertaking. Laid out

by retired Ming imperial official Wang Xianchen in 1513, the three main areas are linked by pools and ponds of varying sizes. Twisting rock-lined paths burst open on to a classical landscape: an expansive lotus pond with a view of the North Temple Pagoda, the pond crossed by zigzag bridges and pavilions perched on hillsides and in hollows.

Follow the signs to the **Garden Museum**. The four exhibition halls tell the story of the classical garden in China and feature a very interesting section on garden construction.

SUZHOU MUSEUM

Exit the museum on Dongbei Jie and head west. At the end of the block is the impressive **Suzhou Museum** ❹ (Suzhou Bowuguan; 204 Dongbei Lu; Tue–Sun

Chinese gardens

The classical Chinese garden is a complex, nuanced thing. In the pavilions, rockeries, fish pools, delicate blossoms and gnarled trees and shrubs are expressions of Chinese poetry, philosophy and art – each garden is supposed to be a microcosm of the world. The pine trees, for instance, symbolise long life, the goldfish money, the peony blooms nobility. Rocks and ponds always feature prominently – and no wonder. After all, the Chinese word for landscape is *shanshui* – literally, mountain water.

A less than humble garden

Exhibit at the Suzhou Silk Museum

9am–5pm, no admission after 4pm; free). The design by Chinese-American architect IM Pei, whose ancestors owned Lion Grove Garden, drew on the ancient city for inspiration. The US$40 million building is a spectacular Modernist version of a traditional Suzhou house, with plenty of glass and light, plus traditional touches such as a Chinese garden and footbridge. The museum features a collection of artefacts from early Suzhou.

OTHER SUZHOU SIGHTS

From the museum, head west on Xibei Jie to the intersection with Renmin Lu and **North Temple Pagoda ❺** (Beisi Ta; 652 Renmin Lu; daily 7.45am–6pm; charge). This 76m (250ft) mustard-and-red structure on the site of Wu Kingdom ruler Sun Quan's childhood home was first built during the third century and rebuilt in the 16th century. A climb to its summit offers spectacular views of the surrounding area – and shows how fast Suzhou is changing.

Cross Renmin Lu to the **Suzhou Silk Museum ❻** (Suzhou Sichou Bowuguan; daily 9am–4.30pm; charge), which recounts the history of silk in China. Especially interesting are the rare antique silk pieces and the section on sericulture: one room has large woven pans holding wriggling silkworms (in season) feasting on mulberry leaves, while on another shelf silk cocoons sit neatly in rows. Weavers demonstrate how young girls ruined their hands in the old days by plunging them

into boiling water to separate the cocoon threads into single strands.

New Suzhou has expanded on either side of the Old Town. **Suzhou Industrial Park (SIP)**, a cooperation between the Chinese and Singaporean governments, fans out to the east around Jinji Lake and is home to high-end hotels, restaurants and nightlife, especially in the lakeside Ligongdi district, filled with whitewashed, heritage-style buildings and bridges.

Food and Drink

❶ PAN PACIFIC SUZHOU

Suzhou Wugong Zhi Taipingyang Jiudian; 259 Xinshi Lu; tel: 512 6510 3388; www. panpacific.com/suzhou; breakfast daily 6.30–10am; $$

The Pan Pacific buffet breakfast offers an impressive array of Asian and Western food, with floor-to-ceiling windows overlooking the hotel's gorgeous classical garden.

❷ SONG HE LOU (PINE AND CRANE RESTAURANT)

72 Taijian Nong; tel: 512 6727 2285; daily 11am–1.30pm, 5–8.30pm; $$

Suzhou's most famous restaurant, where Emperor Qianlong is said to have dined, is a good place to sample Suzhou specialities such as squirrel Mandarin fish, crystal shrimp, Gusu marinated duck, braised river eel and more. The restaurant gets crowded with tourist groups at lunchtime, so come early (11am) or late (1pm).

Hangzhou's West Lake at sunset

HANGZHOU

Hangzhou is a classical Chinese beauty. Its centrepiece is the magical West Lake, and its islands and pavilions, but the city is also home to ancient temples, tea-growing villages and stylish modern enclaves.

DISTANCE: 16–20km (10–12.5 miles), walking and taxis
TIME: Two days
START: Bai Causeway, West Lake
END: Museum of Chinese Medicine
POINTS TO NOTE: The frequent high-speed train service from Shanghai will get you to Hangzhou in under an hour. Once here, you can get around by taxi or hire a car. If you're a fan of tea, come in April to taste the first of the new crop of Hangzhou's famous Longjing tea.

Hangzhou was built on wealth, earned by its fortuitous position as the southern terminus of the Grand Canal and by royal privilege as China's imperial capital during the Song Dynasty. It quickly became an important centre for the silk industry and, as a favourite retreat for China's emperors, it was a place where the noble arts and leisure were cherished. Cycles of destruction – the Taiping Rebellion, which razed the city in 1861, and the Cultural Revolution from 1966 to 1976 – have been interspersed with periods of prosperity, and today Hangzhou is on the up again.

WEST LAKE SIGHTS

Boat tours are an ideal way to see Hangzhou's legendary **West Lake** (Xi Hu) and its attractions. Row yourself or hop aboard a junk, a relaxing way to get a perspective on the lake. The boat ride will take you past Mid-Lake Pavilion and Ruan Yuan's Mound, and you can disembark at Xiao Ying Island. Here, you'll be able to see one of the legendary views of West Lake, a trio of 17th-century stone pagodas floating on the lake called Three Pools Mirroring the Moon. Disembark and head to the northern section of the lake and the **Bai Causeway** ❶ (Bai Di), named after one of Hangzhou's poet-governors, Bai Juyi. Hangzhou's famous **Broken Bridge** (Duan Qiao) stands at the entrance, so-called because when the winter snow on the bridge melts, it appears as if it has been split in two. The bridge is a favourite tourist sight, famous as the setting for the folk tale of Lady White Snake.

Seated Buddhas in Lingyin Temple

Continue south on Bai Causeway to the **Autumn Moon on a Calm Lake** pavilion (Pinghu Qiuyue), much depicted in paintings and one of the traditional spots from which to view the lake. A small road to the right leads to **Crane Pavilion** (Fanghe Ting), built in 1915 in memory of the Song Dynasty poet Lin Hejing, who is said to have lived here alone with only a crane for company.

Just to the west of Autumn Moon on a Calm Lake pavilion, stop for lunch at **Lou Wai Lou**, see ①, Hangzhou's most famous restaurant, with stupendous lake views and delicious classic Hang-zhou dishes – make sure you reserve in advance.

GU SHAN ISLAND

Bai Di causeway connects the mainland with **Gu Shan Island** (Gushan Dao), home to the impressive **Zhejiang Provincial Museum** ② (Zhejiang Sheng Bowuguan; 25 Gushan Lu; Tue–Sun 9am–5pm; free). Built in 1929 in the Modernist Sino-Western 'Nanjing Decade' architectural style, the library is located on the lush grounds of Ming Emperor Qianlong's palace, when the

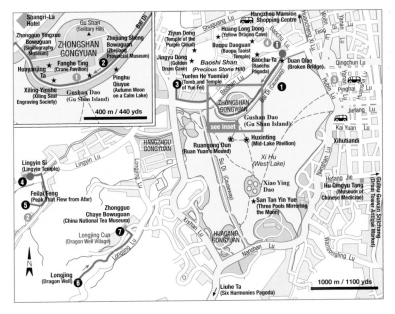

Traditional seals on display

capital was in Hangzhou. The seven halls hold more than 100,000 cultural relics; highlights include the renowned Celadon Hall.

A short walk west is the **Xiling Seal Engraving Society** (Xiling Yinshe; 8.30am–4.30pm; free), with fascinating exhibitions of seals through the ages displayed in pavilions dotted along the hillside. Head behind the Society buildings, up the worn path to the 11-storey unrestored **Pagoda of Avatamsaka Sutra** (Huayanjing Ta), built in 1924. The pagoda and surrounding area is a delightfully quiet spot where locals come for a cup of tea. Surrounded by trees, it makes a lovely place for a break.

Head back down to Gu Shan's southern gate, where you'll find the **Sigillography Museum** (Zhongghuo Yingxue Bowuguan; daily 8.30am–4.30pm; free). The small, very modern museum recounts the history of the Chinese seal, with displays ranging from clay shards to tiny carved seals.

TOMBS AND TEMPLES

Nearby is the **Tomb and Temple of Yue Fei ❸** (Yuefen He Yuemiao; west of Beishan Lu; daily 7am–6pm; charge), a memorial to the 12th-century Song patriot commander who, despite his success against invaders from the north, was framed, arrested and killed with his son Yueyang on trumped-up charges. He was exonerated and given a proper burial 21 years after his death,

in 1163. No longer a functioning temple, its main hall is dominated by a Yue Fei statue with a plaque in Chinese that reads: 'Recover our lost territories' (a reference to Taiwan). Eight murals tell the story of Yue Fei's life. Laid out as a Song Dynasty garden, the temple is connected to the tomb grounds. The back of the temple leads to the **Temple of the Purple Cloud** (Ziyun Dong), the oldest natural cave on the ridge. From here, it's a pleasant walk into the peaceful surroundings of Precious Stone Hill (Baoshi Shan), with views of the 10th-century Baochu Pagoda (Baochu Ta) to the east.

End your day by taking a taxi to **Xihutiandi**, a restaurant, shopping and entertainment complex set in a collection of handsomely refurbished buildings that sit on the eastern shore of West Lake. This is Hangzhou's answer to Shanghai's Xintiandi and, like Xintiandi, it provides an upscale experience coupled with the charm of an authentic local setting.

LINGYIN TEMPLE

Begin your second day at one of China's most famous temples: **Lingyin Temple ❹** (Lingyin Si; 1 Fayun Lane; daily 5am–6pm; charge), or 'Temple of the Soul's Retreat', tucked into the hills west of West Lake. This is Hangzhou's second-biggest attraction after West Lake, so try to visit early in the day to escape the worst of the crowds. The remains of the Indian monk who built the temple in AD 326 are in the sev-

Lingyin Temple

en-storey Liugong Pagoda (Liugong Ta) at the entrance.

One of China's five famous Chan (Zen) sect Buddhist temples, Lingyin has been rebuilt several times, but remarkably it was spared during the Cultural Revolution. This makes it one of the few genuinely ancient temples left in China, and it contains some of the country's rarest relics. These include the lovely 10th-century stone pagodas in front of the Hall of the Four Heavenly Kings. Inside, an 800-year-old statue of Skanda, the Guardian of Buddhist Law and Order, protects an image of the Maitreya (Future) Buddha. Go through the temple, exit via the rear door and cross the courtyard to the Grand Hall. Here, you'll find China's largest sitting Buddha: a 20m (65ft) gilded statue of Sakyamuni Buddha. This 1956 replica of a Tang Dynasty statue is carved from 24 blocks of gilded camphor wood.

FEILAI FENG

From the temple, follow the signs directly south to the evocatively named **Peak That Flew from Afar ❺** (Feilai Feng), so named because founding Indian monk Huili exclaimed that it looked so much like one in India that it must have flown here. It's easy to see his point: Feilai Feng is smaller than the neighbouring sandstone peaks.

Its origins aside, Feilai Feng's main attraction is its stone carvings on the rock face. The 240 mostly intact carvings date

from the 10th century to the 14th century, with the oldest ones being the 10th-century Guanyin (Goddess of Mercy) in the Deep Dragon Cave (Longhong Dong) and the carvings in Shot of Gleam Cave (Shexu Dong). But the favourite is the famous fat, jolly Laughing Buddha.

Follow the path west and the signs to Fayun Village, past the Temple of Goodness (Yongfu Si). This village has been luxuriously refurbished as the home of the **Amanfayun** resort where you can have lunch, see ❷, followed by a traditional tea ceremony featuring Hangzhou's famous Longjing tea at the Teahouse. Take a moment and wander through the complex of restored village houses – it's eminently luxurious, and the meticulous restoration of the thatched roofs and stone walls against the age-old landscape of mountains and ancient trees evoke the charm of old China.

DRAGON WELL VILLAGE

The Amanfayun staff can order a taxi to take you to your next destination: **Dragon Well Village** (Longjing Cun), beginning at the **Dragon Well ❻** (Longjing) itself. Hangzhou's renowned tea of the same name comes from this idyllic mist-laced village atop Longjing Hill. The Dragon Well is composed of two levels of springs that feed the pond creating a line when the water is disturbed, instead of the usual concentric circles. The pure water is said to improve the complexion – which is why you'll see visitors splash-

At the Tomb and Temple of Yue Fei

ing their faces with the cool water. The annual tea harvest occurs in April when you can pick leaves fresh from the terraced fields and have farmers gently dry your harvest in roadside woks.

From Dragon Well, follow Longjing Lu north about 3km (2 miles) downhill, past the pretty tea terraces in the village to the **China National Tea Museum** ❼ (Zhongguo Chaye Bowuguan; Longjing Lu; Tue–Sun 8.30am–4.30pm; free), just north of the village proper. The museum does an excellent job of documenting the history and culture of tea production in its five buildings. Be sure to visit the beautifully decorated tea rooms of the different ethnic minorities, one of the highlights here.

From the museum, take a taxi southeast to the lovely **Six Harmonies Pagoda** (Liuhe Ta; daily 6am–6.30pm; charge; ask the taxi to wait for you). The pagoda, which stands near the northern bank of the Qiantang River, was built in 970 in the hope that it might control the river's mighty tidal waves (it has been unsuccessful). It was last rebuilt in 1900, but the interior dates to 1123. The Song Dynasty pagoda may not have managed to stop the massive tides, but it is still the traditional spot from which to watch the famous tidal bore when a wall of water surges as high as 6m (20ft) down the Qiantang River during the autumn equinox in mid-September.

Continue onwards via car to **Hefang Jie**, on the eastern side of West Lake. This shopping street has recreated a Qing Dynasty setting; shops sell traditional local snacks, plus Chinese knickknacks and souvenirs.

Just off Hefang Jie is the gorgeous **Museum of Chinese Medicine** (Hu Qingyu Tang; daily 8.30am–5pm; charge), a Qing-era building that is a working pharmacy and clinic, reputedly the oldest in China. Despite the name, there isn't much to the museum aside from a few signs (in Chinese), but go in to see the period architecture, pretty courtyards, ornate carving – and the doctors going about their business as they have done for a century.

Hangzhou's top evening attraction is **Impression West Lake** (www.hzyxxh.com) a dazzling music, dance and laser pageant created by Chinese film director Zhang Yimou and performed nightly right on the surface of West Lake. The 70-minute extravaganza is based on Legend of White Snake, a well-loved (and rather tragic) West Lake fairytale set in the Southern Song Dynasty. A 1,800-seat amphitheatre and wooden boat are set up on the banks of the Yuehu Lake Scenic Area (get a seat in the centre of the amphitheatre for best views), and the lake itself becomes a moonlit stage against a backdrop of real-life pagoda-studded mountains.

XIXI NATIONAL WETLAND PARK

West Lake isn't Hangzhou's only watery attraction. In the city's west, the **Xixi National Wetland Park** (Xihu; charge) covers 11.5 sq km of marshy wilder-

T'ai chi in the morning mist

Dragon Well Tea Park

ness. Designated China's first national wetland park in 2005, it offers cruises through the winding waterways that are home to 90 species of migratory birds. You can alight at various stops en route to wander along nature trails lined with mulberry, hibiscus and persimmon trees, go freshwater fishing, and explore the low-lying farming villages, nunneries and noblemen's residences.

DINNER BY WEST LAKE

If it's time for dinner, head to the eastern shore of West Lake for superior local cuisine at **28 Hubin Road**, see ❸, or if you are craving non-Chinese food, venture to the north of West Lake for a meal at **Angelo's**, see ❹, a trendy Italian spot.

Food and Drink

❶ LOU WAI LOU

30 Gushan Lu; tel: 571 8796 9023; www. louwailou.com.cn; daily 9am–10pm; $$
Hangzhou's most renowned restaurant may be packed with tourists, but it still features some of the most well executed local treats in the city, such as beggar's chicken and Dongpo pork – all with a truly unbeatable view of West Lake.

❷ AMANFAYUN

22 Fayun Nong, Xihujiedao Xihufengjingmingsheng District; tel: 571 8732 9999; www.amanresorts.com; $$$$
Amanfayun has several restaurants in smartly refurbished village houses, including a high-end Western restaurant serving a gourmet selection of international dishes that change with the season, a casual steam house showcasing local village-style dishes, a vegetarian house taking cues from the nearby Zen temples and a teahouse offering classic tea ceremonies. It's a relaxing spot after a morning of sightseeing.

❸ 28 HUBIN ROAD

Hyatt Regency Hangzhou, 28 Hubin Road, tel: 571 8779 1234 ext 2828; hangzhou. regency.hyatt.cn; daily 11.30am–2.30pm, 5.30–10pm, last order 30 mins prior to closing; $$$
Fashionable hotel restaurant beside West Lake serving superb local Hangzhou cuisine – don't miss the Dongpo pork belly, beggar's chicken and vinegar lake carp.

❹ ANGELO'S

No. 6, Lane 2, Baoshi Hill, Baochu Road; tel: 571 8521 2100; www.angelos-restaurant. com; 11am–2pm, 5.30pm–midnight, last orders 11pm; $$
If you fancy a break from local cuisine, Hangzhou's contemporary Italian trattoria, a short drive from West Lake, serves excellent thin-crust pizzas, pastas and other Italian favourites, complemented by a comprehensive wine list and welcoming service.

DIRECTORY

Hand-picked hotels and restaurants to suit all budgets and tastes,
organised by area, plus select nightlife listings, an alphabetical listing
of practical information, a language guide and an overview of the best
books and films to give you a flavour of the city.

Many hotels offer lavish spa treatments

ACCOMMODATION

Since the early 20th century, Shanghai's hotel scene has influenced the city's architectural, social and economic development. Back in the 1930s, the 'Paris of the Orient' epitomised modern sophistication with glamour-laden retreats like the Cathay, Palace, Astor House and Park hotels – inspired in style and substance by New York, London and Paris – which attracted global travellers plus local high society to stay and play.

After a long hiatus following World War II and Mao's Communist revolution, the 1990s sparked a renaissance in Shanghai hospitality. This continued into the new millennium, as luxury hotel clusters decorated the Lujiazui, People's Square, Nanjing Road and Hongqiao skylines – many boasting prices as elevated as the high-rise room levels, plus sophisticated dining and deluxe spas.

Shanghai has surged to the top of the global hotel scene, as most of the world's finest international chains have hurried to open brand-new flagship properties in this mega city. They are joined by Asia's top serviced apartment companies, which offer more space, and kitchens, along with some hotel-style services. Many Chinese operators have pitched in with fine properties of their own, some of them in heritage buildings, or in villa compounds with spacious grounds.

The pace of development remains unrelenting. High-profile architects and wealthy developers are teaming up to reconstruct the Pudong and Puxi landscapes with glassy 'mixed use' skytowers, comprising hotels, retail and office space. At the same time, heritage properties along the Bund and in the former French Concession are being converted into more atmospheric, period-infused boutique hotels, while cutting-edge contemporary interiors define a growing band of small design-led hotels.

None of these come cheap, of course. Shanghai is an expensive place to bed down and demand for accommodation still outstrips supply, so book early. Visitors on a lower budget need not fear, however. Shanghai also boasts Asia's fastest growing budget hotel portfolio, most of which are well located and can be booked online.

In general, the quality of accommodation in Shanghai is very impressive. Most of these hotels have opened in the last decade and come equipped

Price for a double room for one night without breakfast:
$$$$ = over RMB 1200
$$$ = RMB 900–1200
$$ = RMB 600–900
$ = below RMB 600

Astor House Hotel on the Bund

The Fairmont Peace Hotel's striking ceilings

with latest technology and competitive guest perks. Large flat-screen TVs, iPod docks, sweet-smelling bath products and rainforest showerheads are found in most of the star-rated hotels. And many Shanghai hotels offer complimentary WiFi and broadband Internet. Service ranges from exemplary to exasperating – but everyone is generally very polite and well meaning. Booking websites www.ctrip.com and www.elong.net offer easy booking and competitive prices.

The Bund

Astor House Hotel (also called Pujiang Hotel)

15 Huangpu Road; tel: 6324 6388; www.pujianghotel.com; $

One of Shanghai's oldest – and best-value – hotels. Albert Einstein, Ulysses S Grant, Bertrand Russell and Charlie Chaplin are all said to have stayed, and it was home to the first electric lights in China. The atmospheric old building just north of the Bund is ripe for a revamp, but stay before that happens because for now this wonderful old gem is still in a reasonably authentic state and offers good value for money. Rooms differ greatly – from stark to ornate.

Captain Hostel

37 Fuzhou Road; tel: 6323 5053; www.captainhostel.com.cn; $

A great location near the riverfront and a few minutes from Nanjing Road. Accommodation ranges from basic 'Sailor Bunks' to standard rooms. Even if you don't stay, the rooftop Captain's Bar, with its Pudong views and cheap drinks, is a welcome antidote to the glitz of its flashier neighbours.

Fairmont Peace Hotel

20 Nanjing Road East, corner Nanjing Road and the Bund; tel: 6321 6888; www.fairmont.com/peacehotel; $$$$

Shanghai's most famous hotel, dating back to 1929, has a striking Art Deco façade and iconic green copper dome. After a three-year makeover, the hotel was finally restored to its former glory in 2010. Although the rooms are small for the price tag, the place is dripping with history.

Hotel Indigo Shanghai on the Bund

585 Zhongshan East No. 2 Road; tel: 3302 9999; www.shanghai.hotel indigo.com; $$$

This 30-storey, 184-room hotel is so close to the water that it feels like you're floating, and it stands out for its sweeping views and deft local design touches, plus a winning rooftop bar and steakhouse. It's on the South Bund, a short taxi hop to the Bund proper and close to the Old Town.

Les Suites Orient Bund Shanghai

1 Jinling Road East; tel: 6320 0888; www.lessuitesorient.com; $$$$

Room with a view at the Peninsula hotel

Located on the South Bund, overlooking the old buildings and river, this is one of Shanghai's most sophisticated stays. Decorated in nutmeg marble and hardwoods, the rooms feature two TVs, free smartphone, a window-front rocking chair, rainforest shower, and free Wifi. There's also a gym and a guest library lounge serving tea and refreshments.

Peninsula Shanghai

32 Zhongshan East No. 1 Road; tel: 2327 2888; www.peninsula.com; $$$$

At the head of the Bund, the stone edifice that houses the Peninsula is half a century younger than its illustrious neighbours, but this exquisite five-star hotel has a timeless Art Deco ambience. Rooms are packed with high-tech luxuries such as internet phones and humidifier controls.

Waldorf Astoria Shanghai on the Bund

No. 2 The Bund, Zhongshan East No. 1 Road; tel: 6322 9988; www.waldorfastoria shanghai.com; $$$$

Housed in a neoclassical Bund building that served as a British gentlemen's club in the 1920s, this exquisite five-star opened in 2010 and features modern-day comforts in a timeless setting. Don't miss a tipple at the Long Bar, a legendary Shanghai drinking institution.

The Waterhouse at South Bund

Nos. 1–3 Maojiayuan Road, Zhongshan Road South; tel: 6080 2988; www.water

houseshanghai.com; $$$$

Set in a 1930s dockyard factory beside the Huangpu River on the South Bund, this 19-room designer hotel features industrial-glam interiors and an excellent Mediterranean restaurant, Table No. 1.

The Westin Bund Centre

88 Central Henan Road; tel: 6335 1888; www.starwood.com; $$$

Its readily recognisable pineapple-shaped crown is visible across the city, and the hotel is equally well known for its landmark Sunday brunch, which features choices from every corner of the globe, spiced up with Chinese dancers, acrobats and jugglers. A comfortable and well-placed choice between the Bund and People's Square.

Suzhou Creek and Hongkou

Banyan Tree Shanghai On The Bund

19 Gongping Road; tel: 2509 1188; www.banyantree.com; $$$$

Far-flung 'urban retreat' with a 130 muted guestrooms, all offering great views along the river – from the pool-size dipping tub in some rooms. There's also an excellent Banyan Tree Spa and a rooftop bar. Not very conveniently placed to the downtown action.

Chai Living

406 North Suzhou Road, Hongkou; tel: 5608 6051; http://chailiving.com; $$$$

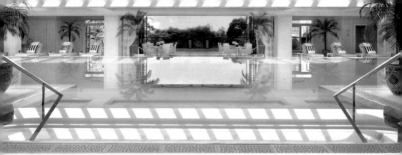

The Peninsula's pool terrace

A collection of serviced residences in the historic Embankment Building on Suzhou Creek. Although the location is slightly out of the way and the building a little rundown, the designer residences offer a rare opportunity to live amongst locals with all the comforts of home.

Hyatt on the Bund

199 Huangpu Road; tel: 6393 1234; www.shanghai.bund.hyatt.com; $$$

When it opened in 2007, this funky riverfront property became the first five-star hotel in the up-and-coming Hongkou district, just north of the Bund. Xindalu restaurant serves the city's best Peking duck, and the top-floor bar and many of the rooms have spectacular views of the Bund and Pudong riverbanks.

Motel 168

300 Huoshan Road; tel: 5117 1111; www.motel168.com; $

One of dozens of Motel 168s in Shanghai, it delivers everything the budget traveller could want: bright, clean rooms, a business centre and free broadband, along with a reliable online reservations system – although only in Chinese – and a bit of spoken English.

Hotel Pravo

299 Wusong Road; tel: 6393 8989; www.hotel-pravo.com; $$

Refined art deco look and feel with elegant rooms in soft pastel tones. Located on the edge of up-and-coming Hongkou district; the tunnel beneath whizzes you to the Bund or Pudong in minutes.

People's Square

JIA

931 Nanjing Road West; tel: 6217 9000; www.jiashanghai.com; $$$$

Singaporean entrepreneur, Yenn Wong, waved her design wand on a Nanjing Road heritage mansion and created a Shanghai icon. Funky, playful and exquisitely styled, Jia offers residence-style rooms with quirky furnishings, kitchenettes and an inbuilt ceiling sound system.

JW Marriott

399 Nanjing Road West; tel: 5359 4969; www.marriotthotels.com/shajw; $$$$

Located atop the iconic Tomorrow Square tower at People's Square, with an elegant main lobby on the 38th floor. Guestrooms feature silk textured wallpaper, mahogany tea chests and marble tubs along with business-oriented amenities. Don't miss JW's Lounge on the 40th floor, which has a 50-strong Martini menu and fine views of the city.

Le Royal Méridien

789 Nanjing Road East; tel: 3318 9999; www.starwood.com; $$$$

At the top of Shimao Plaza, this 333m (1,092ft) 60-storey tower filled with sheared glass and sharp angles opened in 2005 at the corner of People's Park

The pool at Le Royal Méridien

and Nanjing East Road. The interiors are filled with artwork, and the bars and restaurants are shaped by the exterior angles of the building, which give it a unique ambience.

Shanghai Marriott Hotel City Centre

555 Xizang Road Central; tel: 2312 9888; www.marriott.com; $$

Smack-bang central locale just behind People's Square. This smart, functional hotel offers comfort, convenience and connectivity in one large, marble-wrapped package. Great city views and impressive dining at popular chain restaurants, Man Ho (Chinese) and Inagiku (Japanese).

Sofitel Hyland

505 Nanjing Road East; tel: 6351 5888; www.sofitel.com; $$

Located right on busy Nanjing Road, a pedestrianised street between the Bund and People's Square, this four-star hotel has 400 tastefully decorated rooms with comprehensive facilities.

Yangtze Boutique Hotel Shanghai

740 Hankou Road; tel: 6080 0800; $$

So this is what the gilded age looked like: located in a 1934 Art Deco building, this pocket-sized hotel has gorgeous interiors. All rooms feature bold 1930s-style designs coupled with modern technology; some rooms have balconies.

Nanjing Road West

Baolong Home Hotel

125 Nanyang Road; tel: 5174 8188; $

Tucked away behind the Portman Ritz-Carlton, this small-budget hotel is part of a well-managed local chain. Its clean, comfortable rooms and superb location belie the very reasonable rates.

Four Seasons Hotel Shanghai

500 Weihai Road; tel: 6256 8888; www.fourseasons.com/shanghai; $$$

Convenient location straddling the city's two best shopping thoroughfares – Nanjing Road West and Huaihai Road Central. This is one of the older city hotels but comes with stellar Four Seasons service. And don't tell anyone, but it is the top choice of hotel professionals when they travel at their own expense.

Jing An Shangri-La, West Shanghai

1218 Yan'an Road Central; tel: 2203 8888; www.shangri-la.com; $$$$

Part of a massive luxury development beside fashionable Nanjing Road, this 60-storey hotel opened in 2013 and is well placed in Shanghai's fashionable heartlands. Smart, contemporary guestrooms come with top-of-the-city views and there are several excellent restaurants, including Calypso, The 1515 West Chophouse & Bar, and Summer Palace. Jing'an Temple and Park, plus plenty of shopping and dining, lie right on your doorstep.

In the PuLi Hotel & Spa *Shanghai's bedding down options are plentiful*

Pei Mansion Hotel

170 Nanyang Road; tel: 6289 7878;
www.peimansionhotel.com; $$

Revives the stunning 1934 family home of architect IM Pei (who designed the Glass Pyramid at the Louvre). Set in a large garden behind Nanjing Road, the hotel has rooms in faux-classical style with indulgent bathrooms and technology, but patchy service.

Portman Ritz-Carlton

1376 Nanjing Road West; tel: 6279 8888;
www.ritz-carlton.com; $$$

Located in the Shanghai Centre, this recently renovated hotel combines smooth luxury with a location on Nanjing Road, surrounded by a wealth of sightseeing and dining choices.

PuLi Hotel and Spa

1 Changde Road; tel: 3203 9999;
www.thepuli.com; $$$$

Right in the heart of the Puxi CBD, near Nanjing Road and overlooking Jing'An Park, this dazzling hotel has a seductive modern oriental style.

Shanghai Centre

1376 Nanjing Road West; tel: 6279 8600;
www.shanghaicentre.com; $$–$$$$

An excellent and little-known accommodation option within the same complex as the Portman Ritz-Carlton on Nanjing Road West. A genuine bargain, the apartments offer short-term stays in a variety of rooms, from studios to three-bedroom suites.

Swissôtel Grand Shanghai

1 Yuyuan Road; tel: 5355 9898;
www.swissotel.com/shanghai; $$

Well-priced option tucked away behind shopping centres in the fast-changing neighbourhood just north of Nanjing Road. Its key design feature is a grand lobby of polished marble and vaulting gold ceilings, punctuated by a sweeping central staircase.

Urbn

183 Jiaozhou Road; tel: 5153 4600;
www.urbnhotels.com; $$$$

China's first carbon-neutral hotel is far more environmentally friendly than the former factory it replaced. Design-wise, the little boutique property is an effortless success – smooth, minimal and compelling without trying too hard.

Xintiandi and Old Town

88 Xintiandi

380 Huangpi Road South; tel: 5383 8833;
www.88xintiandi.com; $$$$

A refreshing departure from the chain hotels, this boutique residence in the heart of Xintiandi has a charming oriental design, high-tech electronics and kitchenettes. Try to get a room with a balcony.

Andaz Shanghai

88 Songshan Road; tel: 2310 1234;
http://shanghai.andaz.hyatt.com; $$$

Hyatt's hip Andaz brand rises 28 storeys over the heritage rooftops of Xintiandi. Hyper-modern rooms feature

Boutique style

large, cave-like stone bathrooms and high-tech conveniences; you can even choose your own lighting colour scheme. A friendly vibe prevails and guests are encouraged to use the trendy lobby like their living room.

The Langham Xintiandi
99 Madang Road; tel: 2330 2288; xintiandi.langhamhotels.com; $$$$
Supremely elegant hotel in the Xintiandi neighbourhood with polished dark-wood and marble interiors, plus a wonderful Chinese restaurant Ming Court and fashionable outdoor lounge XTD elevated. More dining, nightlife and shopping are at the doorstep.

Oriental Bund Hotel
386 Renmin Road; tel: 6333 8888; www.orientalbundhotel.com; $$
It won't win any style awards, but this mid-level hotel is well priced, with stark but comfortable rooms, a small gym, business centre and a convenient location not far from Yu Garden.

Renaissance Shanghai Yu Garden Hotel
159 Henan Road South; tel: 2321-8888; www.renaissancehotels.com/shasy; $
Overlooking the Old City, this stylish hotel adorned with colourful contemporary interiors and glass sculptures is a well-priced option. Its location close to Yu Garden and the Bund are the main draws. What you shouldn't draw are the curtains at night – the heritage rooftops outlined in yellow light are a magical Shanghai sight.

Shama Luxe at Xintiandi
168 Shunchang Road; tel: 2320 6688; www.shama.com; $$–$$$$
One-, two- and three-bedroom long-stay apartments in styles ranging from traditional to ultra-modern pads. All rooms have fully equipped kitchens, and the property also features a gym, spa, swimming pool and other upmarket hotel features.

Former French Concession

@Gallery Suites
525 Hengshan Road; tel: 5179 5000; www.artgalleryhotels.com; $$
Charming boutique guesthouse in a heritage French Concession residence, with 39 spacious rooms featuring throwback-1930s styling, free-standing bathtubs and modern amenities.

City Hotel
5–7 Shaanxi Road South; tel: 6255 1133; $
Three-star hotel with a great mid-city location, business facilities, Chinese and Western cuisine and a skylit swimming pool.

Hengshan Hotel
534 Hengshan Road; tel: 6437 7050; $$
Formerly the Picardie Mansions, this Art Deco-style hotel is located on tree-lined Hengshan Road. Offers adequate rooms, Western and Chinese

Okura Garden Hotel

restaurants, a business centre and a health club.

Hilton Shanghai

250 Huashan Road; tel: 6248 0000; www.hilton.com; $$$

A venerable hotel that has established itself as an accommodation landmark, the Hilton has a convenient location between the former French Concession and Jing'An Temple. Well managed and always buzzing, it has good restaurants, a skylit pool and penthouse bar.

Howard Johnson Huaihai

1 Fenyang Road; tel: 5461 9898; www.hojochina.com; $

The Howard Johnson fills a key niche: an international-standard hotel that effortlessly delivers all the key amenities at a reasonable price, and with a fine location just off Huaihai Road in the leafy French Concession.

InterContinental Shanghai Ruijin

118 Ruijin No.2 Road; tel: 6472 5222, www.ihg.com/intercontinental; $$$$

Formerly the Ruijin State Guesthouse, this storied property is set within an expansive estate in the heart of the old French Concession dotted with heritage villas, fountains and pavilions. A recent revamp has seen the addition of new buildings with comfortable Chinese-styled guestrooms and a selection of restaurants.

Jin Jiang Hotel

59 Maoming Road South; tel: 3218 9888; www.jinjianghotels.com; $$

The Jin Jiang's buildings were some of the former French Concession's most popular addresses. Rooms are comfortable and homely but not luxurious, with the exception of the Grosvenor House, which offers the most decadent suites at the most decadent prices. Its history trumps the rooms: Richard Nixon and Mao Zedong signed the Shanghai Communiqué here in 1972.

Mansion Hotel

82 Xinle Road; tel: 5403 9888; www.chinamansionhotel.com; $$$$

The Mansion is a grand hotel in miniature, small in stature but large in palatial trappings and old-world charm. The 1920s-era building has just 30 rooms, but its garden courtyard, high-ceilinged lobby and dressy doormen evoke images of classic grandeur, while the rooms feature wood floors, antique mirrors and chandeliered ceilings.

Okura Garden Hotel

58 Maoming Road South; tel: 6415 1111: www.gardenhotelshanghai.com: $$

An old-meets-new property managed by Japan's Okura group, featuring a modern high-rise tower perched adjacent to an historic base: the public areas of the hotel occupy the renovated Cercle Sportif Français (French Club), with many of the historic details and sprawling gardens still intact.

In a Park Hyatt dining area

Taiyuan Villa

160 Taiyuan Road; tel: 6471 6688;
www.ruijinhotelsh.com; $$

This is one of the nicest mansions in the former French Concession, dating back to the 1920s. Taiyuan Villa was once the home of General George Marshall, as well as Mao's dragon-lady fourth wife, Jiang Qing (although not at the same time, of course). Refurbished using 1930s-style Shanghai furniture, the pleasant rooms overlook the villa's sprawling lawns.

Western Shanghai

The Longemont Shanghai

1116 Yan'an Road West; tel: [86-21] 6115 9988 www.thelongemonthotels.com; $$

Despite a rather lackluster location, squeezed up against the Yan'an elevated highway between Hongqiao Airport and downtown, this Chinese-run hotel boasts impressive interiors. With 511 rooms, it can feel busy at peak times, but the comfortable rooms also offer free WiFi.

Xijiao State Guesthouse

1921 Hongqiao Road; tel: 6219 8800;
www.hotelxijiao.com; $$$

What sets this place apart is its picturesque setting in an 80-hectare (200-acre) woodland park. There are stylish rooms as well as villas, the latter for long-term guests and scattered throughout the beautiful grounds. A 20-minute drive from the city centre.

Pudong

Four Seasons Hotel at Pudong

210 Century Avenue; tel: 2036 8888;
www.fourseasons.com/pudong;
$$$$

Sparkling contemporary hotel opened in 2013 on the edge of the Lujiazui. Stylish guestrooms with views over Pudong along with excellent Chinese and Western restaurants. The Spa is well worth a visit, and the swimming pool overlooking Pudong appears straight out of a James Bond movie.

Jumeirah Himalayas Hotel

1108 Meihua Road, Pudong; tel: 3858 0855; www.jumeirah.com; $$$$

Incorporated into the eye-catching Himalayas Art Centre, this cavernous hotel is themed on modern-meets-classical Chinese art. The lobby is dominated by a hand-carved opera pavilion hosting regular performances, and all artworks are original. The rooms have hardwood floors, Ming-style furnishings and high-end technology. Among the eateries is J-Mix, a sleek sushi and teppanyaki restaurant.

Kerry Hotel Pudong

1388 Huamu Road, Pudong; tel: 6169 8888; www.shangri-la.com; $$$$

Shangri-La's luxury business hotel brand dominates the Kerry Parkside complex near Pudong's MagLev station. This vast 574-room hotel features seven floors dedicated to Club accommodation, with

A welcome sight for a weary traveller

24-hour butlers and Club lounge access. A unique highlight popular with all ages is Kerry Sports, Shanghai's largest hotel-based sports club, which features a 24-hour gym, indoor swimming pool, tennis courts and even a rooftop garden with jogging track.

Mandarin Oriental Pudong, Shanghai

111 Pudong Road South; tel: 2082 9888; www.mandarinoriental.com/shanghai; $$$$

Stylish 2013 addition to the Pudong waterfront. Makes up for its lack of centrality with peaceful riverfront gardens, luxurious guestrooms and showpiece dining. Shanghainese restaurant Yong Yi Ting is one of the city's finest. Sunset cruises depart from the luxury marina next door.

Marriott Executive Apartments Union Square

506 Shangcheng Road, Pudong; tel: 2899 8888; www.marriot.com; $$$$

Well-equipped and stylish serviced apartments ideal for short-term stays. The price is similar to nearby high-end hotels, but guests get a separate bedroom, kitchen, living room and other apartment-style perks.

Park Hyatt Shanghai

100 Century Avenue; tel: 6888 1234; www.parkhyattshanghai.com; $$$$

Shanghai's highest hotel, on the 79th–93rd floors of the Shanghai World Financial Centre, is an exclusive retreat above the clouds, with chic, minimalist guestrooms and excellent restaurants.

Pudong Shangri-La

33 Fucheng Road; tel: 6882 6888; www.shangri-la.com; $$$$

A fine five-star with a superb location, the Shangri-La has spacious rooms, first-class service, good views and some of the best dining in the city, along with a superior on-site Chi Spa. Hint: try the Himalayan Bath.

Ramada Pudong Airport

1100 Qihang Road; tel: 3849 4949; www.ramadaairportpd.com; $$

Close to the gateway Pudong Airport, this hotel is a boon for travellers with tight flight connections. There is a full range of restaurants and a health club, and all the TVs receive instant flight information. And don't worry about all those roaring jets – the windows are double-glazed.

The Ritz-Carlton Shanghai, Pudong

8 Century Avenue; tel: 2020 1888; www.ritzcarlton.com; $$$$

Above the Shanghai IFC on the Pudong riverfront, this five-star features a modern Art Deco design, high-tech rooms with magnificent views (reserve a Bund-facing room), plus a stunning alfresco rooftop bar, Flair. There's also an excellent shopping mall and a metro station in the basement.

Shanghai–style bean curd with vegetables

RESTAURANTS

Few cities on earth can match Shanghai for its quality and variety of food. Excellent sit-down meals of meat dumplings or soup noodles, served with a pot of hot tea, can be had for handful of loose change. Meanwhile at the high end, the world's top chefs have flocked to the city, where they have opened elegant flagship venues that serve some of the most refined cuisine on the planet. And in the affordable middle lies a rich treasure trove of regional Chinese cuisines and Western selections from around the globe – many of them served in surprising venues that could only be found in Shanghai. Eating out in Shanghai is one of the city's most quintessential activities, and one that visitors will take to with gusto.

The Bund

Capo

5/F, 77 Beijing East Road; tel: 5308 8332; $$$

Fashionable Neapolitan steakhouse by Naples-born, Shanghai-based chef Enzo Carbone. The dining room, in the attic of a 1911 heritage building

> Price for a two-course meal per person, with one drink:
>
> $$$ = over RMB 250
> $$ = RMB 100–250
> $ = RMB 50–150

behind the Bund, is inspired by a basilica, with its 'altar' reserved for two artisan wood-fired ovens turning out Neapolitan pizzas and Capo's signature 600-day grain-fed organic Australian Wagyu steaks.

Colagreco

2/F, Three on the Bund, 17 Guangdong Road; tel: 5308 5396; www.colagreco. asia; $$$

The Argentinian two Michelin-star chef Mauro Colagreco showcases his delicate fine-dining creations and classic Argentinian steaks in a polished, low-lit dining room looking out to the Bund and Pudong. After dinner, party with Shanghai's social set at the adjoining cocktail and live music lounge, Unico (www.unico. cn.com).

El Willy

5/F, South Bund 22, 22 Zhongshan East No.2 Road; tel: 5404 5757; www.el-willy.com; $$$

The infectiously cheerful Catalan chef 'Willy' Trullàs Moreno helms this popular Spanish restaurant, which relocated from the French Concession to a beautiful heritage building on the South Bund. The produce-driven menu steers on the contemporary side, for example 'juicy rice' is served, instead of traditional paella. Bring a big appetite – and a full wallet.

The choice for dining in Shanghai is excellent

Jean Georges

4/F, Three on the Bund, 3 Zhongshan East (No. 1) Road; tel: 6321 7733; www.threeonthebund.com; $$$

This classy Bund institution by celebrity chef Jean-Georges Vongerichten is the epitome of refined elegance, a world of just-right ingredients expertly mixed and matched, and guaranteed to set the taste buds tingling with delightful flavour combinations.

Lost Heaven on the Bund

17 Yan'an East Road; tel: 6330 0967; www.lostheaven.com.cn; $$

You may get lost in the vast, lush interiors of this 'Mountain Mekong' restaurant, which serves recipes and ingredients from Yunnan province, northern Thailand and Burma in a luxurious, three-storey setting near the Bund waterfront.

M on the Bund

7/F, 5 Zhongshan East (No. 1) Road; tel: 6350 9988; www.m-restaurant group.com; $$$

This time-honoured venue has become famous for its honest Australian-inspired cuisine, featuring fresh ingredients and straightforward preparations, served in a classy Bund setting. Book an outdoor table during good weather, and be sure to try the crispy suckling pig and the pavlova. Award-winning M is consistently rated as one of Shanghai's best restaurants – it's a wonderful combination of smart but unfussy

modern European cuisine, warm service and breathtaking Bund views.

Mercato

6/F, Three on the Bund, 17 Guangdong Road; tel: 6321 9922; $$$

Above Jean Georges at Three on the Bund, Jean Georges Vongerichten has unveiled his first Italian inspired outpost. Mercato's rustic menu, hip concrete and reclaimed wood interiors and comparatively reasonable prices make this an inviting Bund dining destination. The sit-up pizza bar fires gourmet thin-crusts 'til late.

Mr and Mrs Bund

6/F, Bund 18, Zhongshan East (No. 1) Road; tel: 6323 9898; www.mmbund.com; $$$

Shanghai celebrity chef Paul Pairet prepares modern French food with a tiny touch of the unexpected in this Bund 18 hotspot. Behind a big red door, the whimsical interiors with riverfront views set the scene for a memorable Shanghai meal.

Shanghai Grandmother

70 Fuzhou Road (at Sichuan Road); tel: 6321 6613; daily 11.30am–2pm, 6–9.30pm; $

Authentic Shanghai-style home cooking, reputedly from a legendary grandmother's recipe files, in an unstuffy setting. Signature dishes include tender *hongshaorou* (red-cooked pork) and classic *xiaolong bao* (steamed dumplings).

Making xiaolongbao dumplings

Table No. 1

The Waterhouse at South Bund, 1–3 Maojiayuan Road, Zhongshan Road South; tel: 6080 2918; www.tableno-1.com; $$$

Tasty mod-Euro restaurant by London chef Jason Atherton, former frontman for Gordon Ramsay. His first solo venture occupies an industrial-chic 50-seat restaurant in boutique hotel The Waterhouse at South Bund.

Tock's

221 Henan Road Central, 6346 3735; www.tocksdeli.com.cn; $

A tasty pit-stop close to the Bund and Nanjing Road pedestrian street. Shanghai's only Montreal-style deli is renowned for its juicy brisket that they smoke in-house making an incredible reuben. Add a side of the authentic poutine.

Ultraviolet

'Secret' location; book via www.uvbypp.cc; $$$

A truly unique gourmet experience. French chef Paul Pairet (of Mr and Mrs Bund fame, see above) presents a 20-course avant-garde set menu that mixes fine dining with multi-sensorial technologies for just 10 diners each night. Book online.

Xindalu

Hyatt on the Bund, 199 Huangpu Road; tel: 6393 1234; $$$

Shanghai's finest duck comes from the date-wood ovens of this sleek hotel restaurant on the North Bund. Their Beggar's Chicken is also a classic.

Nanjing Road West

Element Fresh

1/F, Shanghai Centre, 1376 Nanjing Road West; tel: 6279 8682; see www.elementfresh.com for other locations; $$

Fresh and healthy American-style café with numerous locations around town. Handy lunch stop with an extensive menu of American and Asian inspired dishes, plus fresh juices, smoothies, all-day breakfasts and good coffee.

Kathleen's 5 Rooftop & Bar

5/F, 325 Nanjing Road West; tel: 6327 2221; www.kathleens5.com.cn; $$

In the old British Racing Club (march past the grumpy guards), this rooftop restaurant occupies a glassed-encased terrace beneath the original clock tower. The Continental menu plays second fiddle to the ambience, but it's a great spot to enjoy a sunset drink with views over People's Park.

Lynn

99-1 Xikang Road; tel: 6247 0101; $

Traditional and updated Shanghainese food in in a smartly styled downtown location. Book ahead for the popular unlimited weekend dim sum brunch.

Qimin Organic Hot Pot

407 Shaanxi Road North; tel: 6258 8777; www.qi-min.com; $$

Lunch at Crystal Jade　　　　　　　　*Frying spring rolls*

Ambience is not usually associated with hotpot restaurants, but this place is a happy exception. In addition to sourcing organic ingredients for the menu, the Taiwanese owners take special care to make sure the broths are superb and not flavoured with MSG. Reservations recommended.

Spice Spirit

7/F, Westgate Mall, 1038 Nanjing Road West; tel: 6217 1777; $

It claims to serve the spiciest food in town, and who could argue? The excellent beef with cayenne pepper and spicy pot chicken wings will have you crying for a cold pijiu (beer). The nightclub-style décor is just as electric.

The Commune Social

511 Jiangning Road; tel: 6047 7638; $$$

Award-winning tapas, dessert and cocktail bar by British celeb chef Jason Atherton. Serves creative small plates designed for sharing in a simple but sleek setting refashioned from a Concession-era police station, with a cute alfresco courtyard. After savouries, you can relocate to the dessert bar or slim upstairs cocktail bar.

Vegetarian Lifestyle

258 Fengxian Road; tel: 6215 7566; $

Also known as Zaozi Shu, this popular spot has an all-vegetarian menu of Chinese dishes. The 'duck' and 'beef' dishes look like the real thing, but are in fact made from tofu or mushrooms.

Yang's Fry Dumpling

2/F, 54–60 Wujiang Road, near Maoming Road; $

Shanghai's favourite haunt for its trademark pan-fried snack, *sheng jian mantou* dumplings. Be prepared to queue at busy times but you can watch the dumplings being made while you wait. Filled with pork and hot broth, they are shallow-fried in wide black pans. There is an art to eating these: take a small bite of the skin first to let the steam escape and carefully suck out the scalding soup before dipping in black vinegar and popping the whole dumpling in your mouth.

Old Town

Lubolang

115 Yuyuan Road, near Mid-Lake Teahouse, Yu Garden; tel: 6328 0602/6355 7509; $$

This rambling, old-school Shanghainese restaurant has prime views of the Mid-Lake Teahouse, curt but efficient old waiters, and a menu filled with Shanghainese favourites, including lion's-head meatballs, red-cooked pork and steamed pomfret.

Nan Xiang

85 Yuyuan Road, near Mid-Lake Teahouse, Yu Garden; tel: 6355 4206; $

A packed three-storey venue with a reputation for serving the best steamed

Uighur bread, made by a Shanghainese minority group

xiaolongbao dumplings in town. There's a takeout on the first floor, a sit-down diner on the second serving basic dumplings, and more elaborate variations (eg crab roe) on the top floor. Reserve ahead so you can enjoy the dumplings in the setting of the third floor.

Xintiandi

Crystal Jade

2/F, South Block, Lane 123 Xinye Road; tel: 6385 8752; www.crystaljade.com; $$

Crystal Jade, of which this is one of several branches, features Shanghainese and Cantonese offerings served in an upscale setting. Try the excellent *dim sum treats*, *dan dan mian* (spicy noodles in peanut sauce) and *jie lan* (a steamed southern vegetable).

Din Tai Fung

2/F, No. 6 South Block Xintiandi, Lane 123, Xingye Road; tel: 6385 8378; $$

The house special is Shanghai's signature dumpling, *xiaolong bao*, steamed dumplings filled with pork, ginger, garlic and a scalding broth. The New York Times hailed the original in Taiwan one of the world's 10 best restaurants.

Soahc

Bldg 3, South Block, Lane 123 Xingye Road; tel: 6385 7777; $$

Taiwanese owner Lily Ho was once a famous Hong Kong movie star, who later resurfaced as a restaurateur with this beautifully designed venue. Specialities include an exceptional, melt-in-your mouth lion's-head meatball with crab meat, while the lotus root appetiser and the subtly spicy Sichuan smoked duck are superb.

Urban Soup Kitchen

280 Madang Road; tel: 3331 1861; www.urbansoupkitchen.com; $

This unpretentious lunch spot, with a few locations, serves some of the best soup and sandwiches in town. The formula is simple – fresh ingredients, no preservatives, triple-filtered water – and they deliver, too, if you get hungry in your hotel room.

Xin Ji Shi

Bldg 9, North Block, Lane 123 Xingye Road; tel: 6336 4746; $$

Xin Ji Shi has multiple outlets serving classic local cuisine: rich stewed pork ribs, crab-egg tofu, lion's-head meatballs and all the rest. The Xintiandi branch is considered to be the best in the city.

Former French Concession

Cantina Agave

291 Fumin Road and Changle Road; tel: 6170 1310; www.cantinaagave.com; $$

A colourful cantina with a sunny pavement patio serving Mexican staples washed down with strong margaritas and 53 tequilas by the glass.

Charmant

1418 Central Huaihai Road, near Fuxing

Artfully displayed tea-cups   *Elegant dim sum presentation*

Road; tel: 6431 8107/6431 8027; $$
Serves Taiwanese comfort food, such as oysters in black bean and scallion, taro cakes, spicy pork with young bamboo shoots, in a city-centre location. Stays open late.

Cha's

30 Sinan Road, near Huaihai Road;
tel: 6093 2062; $
Straight out of old Kowloon, this cute 1950s-styled 'canting' churns out canto classics – soup noodles, roast chicken, milk tea – until 2am each day. Be prepared to queue.

Cheng Cheng's Art Salon

164 Nanchang Road, near Sinan Road; tel: 6328 0602; $$
This cosy, art-filled salon is both a restaurant and a gallery, with eye-catching décor, as might be expected. The food served is equally out-of-the-box Shanghainese and Sichuan fare, free of MSG.

Chun

124 Jinxian Road, near Maoming Road;
tel: 6256 0301; $–$$
Chun is like eating in the home of a Chinese grandmother: it has four tiny tables, and you eat what the owner, Ms Qu, has bought fresh in the market that day. The offerings are sweet, heavy, oily and unapologetically Shanghainese, such as snails, eel, fish and pork ribs. There are two evening seatings, and reservations are required.

Di Shui Dong

56 Maoming Road, near Changle Road; tel: 6253 2689; $
This fiery favourite specialises in Hunan cuisine (similar to Sichuan, but less well known), and with its rustic decor and boisterous atmosphere, really packs 'em in. The cumin-encrusted ribs are the signature dish. Reserve in advance.

Franck

Ferguson Lane, 376 Wukang Road; tel: 6437 6465; www.franck.com.cn; $$$
French brasserie cuisine, such as beef tartare, confit de canard and roast chicken, that is beautifully executed and served in a casual-chic space complete with brusque French-speaking waiting staff.

Guyi Hunan

87 Fumin Road, near Julu Road; tel: 6249 5628; $$
This sparkling little restaurant, with its monumentally spicy food, is a good place for a lively dinner. The dishes served up at Guyi are more refined and less oily than most of the city's spicy offerings.

Haiku by Hatsune

28B Taojiang Road, by Hengshan Road; tel: 6445 0021; $$–$$$
Japanese treats and cutting-edge decor on one of the old Concession's most charming cobbled streets, surrounded by a wealth of after-dinner drinking

options. The fusion-inspired sushi is bold and original.

Hengshan Café
308 Hengshan Road; tel: 6471 7127; $
This clean, well-lit café features a light, friendly selection of Cantonese and Shanghainese comfort dishes. Start with some barbecue pork or roast duck, and continue with the 'tiger-striped' chilli peppers, stewed ribs, steamed fish and crispy stir-fried vegetables.

Jesse Restaurant
41 Tianping Road, near Huaihai Middle Road; tel: 6282 9260; $$
This charming hole in the wall serves some of the tastiest Shanghainese food in town – red-cooked pork ribs, stir-fried vegetables, steamed fish – as evidenced by the clusters of hungry people waiting outside. A precursor to the fancier Xin Ji Shi restaurants, it is small, plain and unpretentious, but it really is one of the best.

Madison & Madi's
Bldg 2, 3 Fenyang Road; 6437 0136; $$-$$$
Bright and airy dining room filled with happy people chowing down on 'casual fine-dining American' fare by young American-Chinese chef-owner Austin Hu. The adjacent café-restaurant Madi's is a great spot for a relaxed brunch or lunch while exploring the French Concession (see page 52). The duck fat disco fries are awesome.

Maya
No. 2 Bldg, 568 Julu Road, inside the Shanghai Grand Plaza compound; tel: 6289 6889; $$$
This tucked-away Mexican restaurant serves creative versions of time-honoured south-of-the-border favourites, such as lime beef, cilantro chicken and fish tacos, along with generous jugs of sangria.

Mr Willis
3/F, 195 Anfu Road; tel: 5404 0200; $$
Australian chef Craig Willis and his team dish up Oz-Med comfort food for sharing from the open kitchen in this cosy loft restaurant in the former French Concession treetops. Great weekend brunches, too.

Noodle Bull
291 Fumin Road; near Xinle Road; tel: 6170 1299; $
A great option for a quick and tasty lunch, this cool, contemporary noodle joint serves deep bowls of hand-pulled noodles and tasty sides. Wash these down with the house plum juice.

Shintori
803 Julu Road, near Fumin Road; tel: 5404 5252; $$$
Shintori has a beautifully presented bamboo-bedecked entrance that leads to a large, open dining room with an open kitchen that turns out a fine selection of sushi and sashimi, along with updated versions of other Japanese classics.

In Nan Xiang steamed bun restaurant

Sichuan Citizen

30 Donghu Road, near Huaihai Road;
tel: 5404 1235; $$

This upbeat, provincial-chic diner turns out a large picture menu of fresh, well-spiced Sichuan classics, accompanied by a selection of cooling cocktails. A local expat favourite – book ahead.

South Beauty 881

881 Central Yan'an Road; tel: 6247 6682;
southbeautygroup.com/en; $$$

This impressive venue serves first-rate Sichuan food in a lavish century-old mansion and sprawling grounds. The food is genuine, tongue-searing Sichuan; the signature dish is beef cooked at the table in hot spicy oil.

Southern Barbarian

Area E, 2/F, Ju'Roshine Life Art Space,
56 Maoming Road South; tel: 5157 5510;
$$

Tucked away in gritty second-floor space, this bohemian restaurant draws the crowds on account of its authentic Yunnanese cuisine, typified by ingredients like cheese and exotic mushrooms. Try the jizhong mushrooms, fried goat's-milk cheese or clay-pot chicken – you won't be disappointed.

Sushi Oyama

2/F, 20 Donghu Road, near Huaihai Road;
tel: 5404 7705; $$$

Fourteen-seat, reservations-only restaurant with a custom menu that changes nightly, depending on which ingredients the eponymous master chef imports fresh from Japan that day. It features the best sushi this side of Japan, and melt-in-your-mouth kobe beef, along with a selection of fine sakes.

Tsui Wah

291 Fumin Road, near Changle Road;
tel: 6170 1282; $

Part of a small, Hong Kong-based chain, Tsui Wah offers reliable Cantonese favourites, plus a selection of Western dishes and a small bakery.

Yongfoo Elite

200 Yongfu Road, near Fuxing Road;
tel: 5466 2727; $$

Elegant Shanghainese flavours in an exquisitely styled former French Concession garden villa that captures the spirit of Shanghai's 1930s heyday.

Vedas

3/F, 83 Changshu Road; tel: 6445 8100;
www.vedascuisine.com; $$

One of the best Indian restaurants in town, Vedas combines an open kitchen, classy but understated decor and refined versions of many Indian classics, with the Bombay prawn curry and tandoori chicken among the highlights.

Western Shanghai

Ben Jia

1339 Wuzhong Road; tel: 5118 2777;
$$

Obscured from the road by a Hyundai dealersip, Seoul-import Ben Jia

A choice of spirits

is Shanghai's finest Korean barbeque restaurant, not least for the overwhelming tray of fresh leaves and vegetables to wrap it all up in. Waiters hustle through the dining room with an endless parade of *banchan*, the customary *kimchi*, salads and sides, stopping to adjust the thinly sliced beef brisket on your charcoal fire, or deliver another Hite beer.

Dong Bei Ren

46 Panyu Road, near Yan'an Road West; tel: 5230 2230; $

Expect colourful uniforms, singing staff and over-the-top decor, along with rich and hearty meat-and-potatoes cuisine, and Harbin beer that is plentiful and cheap.

Fu 1039

1039 Yuyuan Road, near Jiangsu Road; tel: 5237 1878; $$$

Fu 1039 serves classic Shanghainese specialities in the setting of a tucked-away heritage villa filled with antiques. The sophisticated but relaxed atmosphere projected here makes this restaurant a winner.

Shen Yue Xuan

Ding Xiang Garden, 849 Huashan Road; tel: 6251 1166; $$

Quality Cantonese and Shanghainese cuisine in a pretty garden setting. Qingyuan-style chicken, shrimp dumplings and 1000-year-egg congee and honeyed ribs are among the specialities.

Ye Old Station Restaurant

201 Caoxi Road North; tel: 6427 2233; $$

Only in Shanghai, perhaps, could a former French nunnery be converted into a museum-restaurant filled with old train carriages, in which you can dine. The food is classic Shanghainese, with sautéed fresh shrimp, lion's-head meatballs, stewed pork ribs, and fried and steamed fish from the nearby shallow lakes and rivers.

Pudong

100 Century Avenue

Park Hyatt Shanghai, 91/F, 100 Century Avenue; tel: 6888 1234; www.shanghai.park.hyatt.com; $$$$

This 91st-floor restaurant, with dramatic floor-to-ceiling windows overlooking the cityscape, has something for everyone: a choice of three menus (Western steakhouse, Chinese and Japanese), all served within the same stunning space in the clouds. The show kitchens add a real sense of razzle-dazzle and there are glamorous bars on the 92nd and 93rd floors.

Din Tai Fung

3/F, Super Brand Mall, 168 Lujiazui Road, near Oriental Pearl Tower; tel: 5047 8882; $$

This popular Taiwanese chain serves arguably Shanghai's best *xiao long bao* steamed dumplings, along with a long menu of fresh and clean-tasting regional Chinese favourites. This

The fabulous view from Flair　　　　　　　　　　*A romantic setting at Flair*

Pudong outlet also boasts spectacular river views.

Face

Dongjiao State Guesthouse, 1800 Jinke Road; near Longdong Highway; tel: 5027 8261/3668; www.facebars.com; $$

A superb dining option in far-flung Pudong, this exquisite collection of restaurants in the grounds of Dongjiao State Guesthouse features four cuisines – Thai, Indian, Japanese and North African. There's also the gorgeous Face Bar, where you can sip cocktails on antique opium beds.

Flair

58/F, The Ritz-Carlton Pudong, Shanghai IFC Tower, 8 Century Avenue; tel: 2020 1888; www.ritzcarlton.com; $$$

The city's highest open-air lounge boasts a split-level terrace with spectacular views of the Oriental Pearl Tower and the Bund. Serves gourmet pan-Asian tapas from the outdoor grill, accompanied by creative cocktails and wines. Reserve ahead for one of the popular terrace perches.

The Kitchen Salvatore Cuomo

2967 Binjiang Avenue, near Fenghe Road, Pudong; tel: 5054 1265; $$

A favourite among Italian expats living in Shanghai. Set against the waterfront under the Oriental Pearl Tower, this venue offers good views along with its pizza and perfectly cooked pasta dishes.

Lei Garden

3/F, IFC Mall Pudong, 8 Century Avenue; tel: 5106 1688; $$$

Found in the sleek IFC Mall, an appropriately high-end setting, this branch of Hong Kong's Michelin-starred Cantonese restaurant chain serves exquisite Cantonese classics with a focus on fresh seafood. It also does a brisk business in weekend *yum cha*.

Matto

GF50, Super Brand Mall, 168 Lujiazui Road West; tel: 5081 0966; www.mattopizza.com; $$

At the base of Super Brand Mall in Pudong, this laidback pizzeria and bar by the folks behind high-end steakhouse Capo serves excellent wood-fired Neapolitan pizzas and antipasti, along with a comprehensive menu of wines and cocktails. On a fine day, the wood terrace is a lovely place to sip under the skyscrapers.

Yong Yi Ting

B1/F, Mandarin Oriental Pudong, 111 Pudong Road South; tel: 2082 9978; $$$

Mandarin Oriental's signature Chinese restaurant helmed by Shanghai celeb chef Tony Lu is one of the city's finest destinations to sample local Jiang Nan cuisine – meaning literally, South Yangtze River – which is known for its light and delicate flavours. Also has alfresco tables and an impressive wine list.

Customers enjoy drinks and laughs at the Glamour Bar

NIGHTLIFE

Shanghai's notoriously decadent 1930s nightlife scene entered a prolonged lull following World War II and the 1949 Communist Revolution. Half a century later, in the early noughties, bar and club culture exploded, mirroring China's economic boom. Today, Shanghai's nightlife compares favourably with any hard-partying metropolis.

Midnight is the witching hour in Shanghai, when the city's night owls start to prowl the streets. The clubs and bars of choice change frequently, as newer, bigger and better-designed challengers throw open their doors. The result is a dynamic club culture that is packed with after-dark temptations, ranging from glamorous cocktail bars to DJ-fuelled dance clubs, to crowded live music bars. Shanghai is a party that doesn't stop until the sun peers over the Huangpu River, and sometimes not even then. Get dressed up and make your way to one of the following venues.

Bars and clubs

No. 88
2/F, 291 Fumin Road; tel: 6136 0288
Up a twisting wooden staircase, 88 is an insanely over-the-top Chinese-style dance club with flamboyant furnishings, roving performers and elevated dancefloors. You'll have to buy by the bottle to get a table – the Champagne arrives with flaming sparklers. Drink up and enjoy the unique party atmosphere.

Bar Rouge
7/F, 18 Zhongshan Road East No.1; tel: 6339 1199; www.bar-rouge-shanghai.com
This big Bund 18 hotspot draws upscale crowds with its cranberry-coloured lounges, hot red lighting and professional DJs – despite its famously snooty service. The best tables are on the terrace overlooking the Huangpu River; be sure to reserve or arrive early for an outside perch.

Cirque Le Soir
4/F, 22 Zhongshan East No.2 Road; tel: 400 9910088; http://cirquelesoir.com
High-end circus-themed nightclub from London and Dubai on the Shanghai Bund. Runs the gamut from sexy to surreal with everything from shirtless clowns juggling on stilts to tattooed, scantily clad female axe-throwers.

M1NT
318 Fuzhou Road; tel: 6391 2811; www.M1NT.com.cn
Shark tanks, Bund views, beautiful people and more in this lavish club perched atop a 24-storey building behind the Bund. Entertainments include seasoned DJs, a spacious dance floor, bar, restaurant, rooftop party area and superb modern design. M1NT claims to be

Wall art using beer bottles

members-only, but go before 9.30pm and you will be ushered right in.

Shanghai Studio

Building 4, 1950 Central Huaihai Road, near Wukang Road; tel: 6283 1043; www.shanghai-studio.com

A labyrinthine concrete lair in a former bomb shelter, this popular alternative hangout is known for its friendly staff, stiff drinks, welcoming vibe and over-the-top costume parties. Expect a maze of rooms, many of them featuring off-beat Asian art, a small dance floor, and a mixed local and expat crowd.

The Shelter

5 Yongfu Road, near Fuxing Road West; tel: 6347 0400

Every city needs a nightclub like The Shelter: concrete walls, black paint, rock-bottom drinks prices and consist-ently good music. This basement club draws a youthful alternative crowd, who are joined by locals looking for a good time in unpretentious surroundings.

Unico

2/F, Three on the Bund, 17 Guangdong Road; tel: 5308 5399; www.unico.cn.com

A classy late-night venue at Three on the Bund decked out with giant lan-terns, colourful armchairs and a central bar. Choose from a fun cocktail/tapas menu arranged and paired according to Latin American compass coordinates, and sway to the beats of live Latin musi-cians and guest DJs.

Cocktail lounges

Bar Constellation

251 Huangpi Road North, near Jiangyin Road; tel: 5375 2712

This 1930s-themed cocktail bar is much loved for its fine mixology. Its clas-sic cocktails are perfectly balanced and never too sweet, and whisky and other drinks on the rocks are served 'Japa-nese style' with a single large ice cube, so they stay cold without getting watery.

Glamour Bar

6/F, 5 Zhongshan East (No.1) Road; tel: 6329 3751; www.m-glamour.com

A sophisticated waterfront bar below sister restaurant M on the Bund with a mirrored cocktail bar, champagne bar, wine-tasting table and superior bar bites. Jewel-coloured velvet armchairs, Art Deco lamps and arched windows overlooking the Bund set the elegant ambience.

The Long Bar

6/F, 2 Zhongshan East (No.1) Road; tel: 6322 9988; www.waldorfastoria shanghai.com

This legendary Shanghai watering hole dates back to the 1920s, when it was an exclusive British gentlemen's club with the longest bar in Asia. Noel Cow-ard famously remarked that 'one could see the curvature of the earth along it'. Now part of Waldorf Astoria hotel, the bar has been restored to its former glory and serves well-mixed cocktails, along with fresh oysters from the Oyster Bar.

Shanghai Grand Theatre performance

Live music

LOgO

107 Sinan Road, near Taikang Road;
www.logoshanghai.net

A youthful favourite that is much loved for its consistent presentation of alternative music, including electronic, punk rock and metal, as well as for its gritty, smoky, laid-back interiors and reasonable cover charges. The house is packed at weekends with crowds of 20- and 30-somethings gathered for a good time.

Theatres and concert halls

Mercedes-Benz Arena

1200 Expo Avenue, Pudong; tel: 400 181 6688; www.mercedes-benzarena.com

The oyster shell-shaped performance arena on the Huangpu riverside was built for the 2010 World Expo and is the first in China to have a naming rights deal. A state-of-the-art showplace for culture, arts, sports and entertainment events, it features a multifunctional auditorium hosting everything from rock concerts to basketball games, a Cineplex, ice-skating rink and music club.

Oriental Arts Centre

425 Dingxiang Road, Pudong; tel: 6854 1234; www.shoac.com.cn

This Paul Andreu-designed centre in Pudong has five circular halls that resemble a lotus flower in full bloom. Three theatres – a Concert Hall, Opera Hall and a smaller Performance Hall – all have superb sightlines, state-of-the-art acoustics and nature-inspired designer interiors.

Shanghai Circus World

2266 Gonghexin Road, near Guangzhong Road; tel: 5665 3646

In the city's north, this modern arena with a revolving stage and digital water curtain, hosts *ERA: Intersection in Time*, a multimillion-dollar acrobat/circus show that runs daily.

Shanghai Concert Hall

523 Yan'an Road East; tel: 6386 2836; www.shanghaiconcerthall.org

This venerable hall opened in 1930 as the Nanking Theatre, but in 2002 was relocated brick by brick to a new location just over 50 metres away. The classically styled beauty, now with better acoustics and a roomier stage, showcases a rich selection of performances year-round.

Shanghai Conservatory of Music

20 Fenyang Road; tel: 6431 8542/6431 2157

Students are in the spotlight at the conservatory's He Lu Ting Concert Hall throughout the semester, and performances are open to the public free of charge. Concert schedules vary depending on the courses being offered, and on occasion, visiting musicians from Europe, North America and Asia present performances together with their students.

Shanghai is known for glamour

Smoking indoors is still largely permitted in Shanghai

Shanghai Culture Square

36 Yongjia Road; tel: 5461 9961;
www.shculturesquare.com

This massive underground theatre opened in 2011 in a park in the former French Concession. It stages mostly musical theatre and ballet performances.

Shanghai Grand Theatre

300 People's Avenue; tel: 6372 8702;
www.shgtheatre.com

Opened in 1998 in People's Park, Shanghai Grand Theatre has a striking design that is a modern interpretation of a Chinese hall with upturned eaves that glow from within on theatre nights. It has one of the biggest and best equipped stages in Asia, and plays host to extravagant musicals such as *The Lion King* and *Cats*, while smaller performances are held in cosier side theatres.

Film

Grand Cinema

216 Nanjing Road West; tel: 6327 1899;
www.shdgm.com

Several cinemas across town show movies in English and Chinese (check to confirm when purchasing tickets), but none quite like this iconic venue. The benefit of going to the Grand Cinema on People's Square is that you can also enjoy the fabulous Art Deco architecture of this 1933 movie theatre. There's also a rooftop lounge to enjoy and a mini museum, which is worth a visit.

Jazz venues

House of Blues and Jazz

60 Fuzhou Road, near The Bund; tel: 6323 2779

This gem of a club in a renovated mansion on a quiet Bund backstreet attracts a firm following with its unpretentious but upscale atmosphere and excellent bands that play soul-infused blues and jazz. Its long wood-grained bar, hardwood walls and floors, and Art Deco-style fittings pay tribute to Shanghai's earlier jazz era.

The Jazz Bar

Fairmont Peace Hotel, 20 Nanjing Road East; tel: 6321 6888; www.fairmont.com/peacehotel

A 1930s jazz institution, the dark and intimate Jazz Bar at the Peace Hotel features the original vintage jazz band (all members are aged 70 plus) playing timeless tunes in the early evening, followed by the more upbeat house band and guest performers, playing late into the Shanghai nights.

JZ Club

46 Fuxing Road West; tel: 6431 0269;
www.jzclub.cn

While most 'jazz' venues in Shanghai play pop music and blues and even showtunes, JZ remains true to its roots, with an ongoing selection of superlative jazz musicians from China and overseas, plus a fine house band. A friendly two-storey layout, where listeners are almost on top of the stage. Book early for top bands.

Old and modern Shanghai

A–Z

A

Addresses

Buildings are usually sequentially numbered, odd numbers on one side of the street and even numbers on the other. As the major streets often run the entire length of the city, it helps to know what the nearest cross-street is when trying to locate an address, such as Central Huaihai Road near *(kaojing)* Gao'an Road. It's easier with newer buildings, as the street address now indicates building numbers within an area – for example, Central Huaihai Road 1000–2000.

Age restrictions

It is illegal to sell alcohol and tobacco to those under 18 years of age in China, although the law is not strictly enforced. It is not uncommon for children to be given small amounts of beer or wine at family dinners, and it is relatively easy for teenagers to buy alcohol and cigarettes without ID in shops and clubs.

B

Budgeting

Shanghai is China's most expensive city, although you can still enjoy some good bargains. Accommodation can cost from as little as RMB 100 for a dorm bed to upwards of RMB 3,000 for one of the city's deluxe five-star hotels.

Similarly, a meal in a simple Chinese restaurant can cost as little as RMB 50 per person, while you can easily pay RMB 500 at the one of the city's swankier Chinese or Western eateries. Local beer costs as little as RMB 25; imported beer is three times more. A glass of wine at an expensive restaurant costs RMB 60 and upwards.

The city's efficient public transport system is cheap – a bus or metro ride within the downtown area won't cost more than RMB 5. Taxi rides are also inexpensive, running about RMB 14–30 for trips within the city centre, or slightly more after 11pm, when flag fall starts at RMB 18.

Entry fees to most attractions are under RMB 20, except for prime attractions that can cost around RMB 100. In 2007, many parks and museums stopped charging admission, and provincial art galleries across the country are now following suit. Most temples charge a nominal entrance fee.

Business cards

In business and other formal situations in Shanghai, you will be expected to present a business card. Present cards with both hands, and accept them the same way.

Chinese New Year parade

C

Children

The Shanghainese love children. There is not a museum, restaurant or theatre where your child will feel unwelcome. The downside is a loss of privacy: your kids will be touched, stared at, talked to and photographed – just take a positive attitude about the whole thing and you'll meet new friends and gain fresh insights.

Hotels often allow children to stay with parents in a double room at no extra charge. Extra beds are available for a small surcharge. Reliable babysitters, called *ayi* (aunty), are easily available. If you're planning to be in Shanghai for any length of time, consider a serviced apartment with kitchen and laundry facilities.

Climate

Shanghai has a northern subtropical monsoon climate with four distinct seasons. Rainfall is plentiful throughout the year, though most of it falls during the rainy season from June to September. Expect hot and muggy summers with daytime temperatures hovering in the low to mid-30s°C (90–95°F) in July and August, and chilled-to-the-bone damp winters in December and January. January is the coldest month, with daytime temperatures usually below 10°C (50°F), occasionally dipping below zero at night. Snow is rare in Shanghai, although there are sometimes late December/January flurries.

The city's most comfortable (and sunny) weather is in spring (mid-March to May) and autumn (September to early November), although even then it is hardly reliable.

Clothing

Shanghai errs on the side of casual, but it is a city of unrelenting style: you'll be forgiven for not wearing a tie, but never for looking like a bumpkin. Light, breathable clothes work best in the hot, humid summer months, with a light cover-up for overly air-conditioned restaurants and offices. In winter, several layers of clothing are the key to staying warm – coats, scarves, hats etc. Savvy travellers always carry a foldable umbrella with them to protect against sudden showers.

Crime and safety

Shanghai is a relatively safe city, but petty crimes such as pickpocketing do occur in crowded areas like train stations, markets and busy streets. There is very little violent crime against foreigners, but tourists should be aware of scams that generally begin with a request from the scammer to practise their English or visit a student art exhibition. Avoid unlicensed cab drivers or motorcycle taxis.

Shanghai is a safe city for women, who are able to walk alone, even at night, without being harassed – but again, you should be on your guard.

Migrant workers flock to Shanghai to find work

Every neighbourhood has its own police station or post, often labelled in English. This is the place to report any crime, although you might have to wait for the Public Security Bureau officer in charge of foreigners to handle your case. Otherwise, contact the Public Security Bureau directly.

Customs

Duty-free allowance per adult is as follows: two bottles of liquor (75cl each), 400 cigarettes, 50g of gold or silver, and perfume for personal use. On arrival, tourists have to fill out a baggage declaration form and hand it in to customs. There is no limit to the amount of foreign currency and Chinese Renminbi traveller's cheques that can be brought in; the unspent portion may be taken out.

There is a long list of prohibited items, including animals, firearms, plant material and media deemed 'detrimental' to China's social and political security. For up-to-date details see www.china.org.cn. Note: antiques require a government stamp in order to be exported; most reputable dealers can take care of the necessary paperwork.

Disabled travellers

Most of Shanghai's modern hotels, buildings and museums are wheelchair-accessible, but older buildings and the myriad over/underpasses and walkways can present challenges for disabled travellers. Newer metro stations all have lifts or wheelchair ramps, though you may need to contact staff first to have these activated. Bashi Taxi (tel: 6431 2788) has several minivans that cater for the wheelchair-bound.

Electricity

Local electricity is 220 volts; 50 cycles AC.

Chinese-to-foreign conversion accessories – whether conversion plugs or voltage converters – are easily available at department stores and hotels.

Embassies and consulates

Australia: 22/F, Citic Square, 1168 Nanjing Road West; tel: 2215 5200; www.shanghai.china.embassy.gov.au
Canada: 8/F, Eco City Building, 1788 Nanjing Road West; tel: 3279 2800; www.shanghai.gc.ca
New Zealand: Rm 1605–1607A, The Centre, 989 Changle Road; tel: 5407 5858
Singapore: 89 Wanshan Road; tel: 6278 5566
United Kingdom: Suite 301, Shanghai Centre, 1376 Nanjing Road West; tel: 3279 2000; www.ukinchina.fco.gov.uk
United States: 1469 Central Huaihai Road; tel: 6433 6880

Traffic jams full of taxis are a common sight in Shanghai

Emergencies

The police have a foreign translator on hand 24/7, so their's is the best number to call in an emergency.

Ambulance: 120
Fire: 119
Police: 110

Etiquette

You could be forgiven for thinking that 'anything goes' in Shanghai. But do bear in mind the following:

Shoes should be removed when entering homes; sometimes slippers will be provided.

Use both hands to present business cards at meetings.

Tea should be offered when you host someone, whether at home or in a business setting.

If you invite someone to go for dinner, you're usually expected to pay for the entire meal – the Shanghainese only 'go Dutch' with close friends or their colleagues.

Fortunately, the Shanghainese are very forgiving of foreigners when it comes to local rules of etiquette, so you'll be excused most gaffes with no problems.

The most serious breaches of etiquette tend to involve politics rather than manners: although the atmosphere is far more open now, it's still wise to avoid overtly political discussions, especially involving sensitive topics like Taiwan and Tibet.

G

Gay and lesbian travellers

Acceptance of the gay and lesbian community in Shanghai has been tentative on an official level. Shanghai LGBT (shanghailgbt@yahoogroups.com) hosts events in the city's gay and lesbian bars.

Homosexuality is generally frowned upon in China – it was only downgraded from a mental illness in 2001 – but in liberal Shanghai, the gay scene is increasingly open, albeit a predominantly male one. Nevertheless, discretion prevails; China is still basically a conservative society, so flagrant displays of affection are best avoided.

Green issues

China is one of the world's worst polluters, but environmental concerns are starting to be taken seriously. Air pollution is a serious problem that can cause discomfort on 'bad air' days when the city is blanketed in thick smog. Consider wearing a mask, particularly if you're sensitive. The China Air Quality Index app charts real-time air pollution readings of the dangerous PM2.5 particles in cities across China, and alerts when protection is recommended. On the street level in Shanghai, collecting and recycling waste materials is a means of business for many low-income senior citizens, aided by recycling bins across the city. Cycling is also a popular means of getting around the flat and compact

A trendy store logo

inner city – though can be a dangerous undertaking if you're not familiar with Shanghai's crazy traffic.

China is also leading the way in solar power and other environmental building technologies. The twice-yearly grassroots **Eco Design Fair** champions sustainable producers and healthy lifestyles. Its website, www.ecodesign fair.cn, also serves as a directory and general community resource. For those conscious of their carbon footprint, Shanghai's Urbn Hotel (www.urbnhotels.com) is China's first carbon-neutral hotel – with plenty of style to boot.

H

Health

Healthcare in Shanghai is reasonably good. There are Western-staffed clinics and designated foreigners' clinics in local hospitals with English-speaking personnel. For more serious and complicated issues, patients often return to their home countries or seek treatment in Hong Kong, so visitors to Shanghai are encouraged to have health insurance that covers repatriation expenses. You should bring all required medications during your visit, whether over-the-counter or prescription, as medicines may be sold under different names.

Inoculations

Other than requiring a yellow fever vaccination certificate from travellers coming from tropical South America or sub-Saharan Africa, Shanghai does not require any immunisations.

The Centre for Disease Control (CDC) in Atlanta, US, recommends the following vaccines for travellers to Shanghai (see www.cdc.gov). Be sure to consult your doctor at least four to six weeks before your trip so that there is sufficient time for the shots to take effect:

Hepatitis A – A food- and water-borne viral infection of the liver.

Hepatitis B – An estimated 10 to 15% of the Chinese population carry hepatitis B, which is transmitted through bodily fluids and can lead to liver disease. The vaccine is recommended if you might be exposed to blood, have sexual contact with the local population, stay longer than six months or risk exposure through medical treatment.

Japanese encephalitis – This is only recommended if you plan on visiting rural areas for four weeks or more, except under special circumstances such as an outbreak of the disease.

Rabies – Recommended if there is risk of exposure to wild animals.

Hospitals and clinics

Emergency/evacuation:

SOS International 24-Hour Service, tel: 6295 0099.

Emergency/general:

Shanghai East International Medical Centre, 150 Jimo Road, Pudong; 24hr hotline: 5879 9999, 150 0019 0899. Opened in 2003, this international-class facility is operated by Shanghai

PLC soldiers   *Many cafés offer WiFi*

East Hospital and a California-based healthcare company. Provides both out-patient and in-patient medical services.

Huashan Hospital, 15/F, Foreigners' Clinic, 12 Urümqi Road; tel: 6248 3986. A mid-sized general hospital which offers most specialities.

Parkway Health, Room Nos. 203–4, Shanghai Centre, 1376 Nanjing Road West; tel: 6445 5999; www.parkway health.cn.

Reputable clinic with overseas-trained and English-speaking doctors and staff. Operates clinics throughout the city. For 24-hour assistance, call 6445 5999

Pudong Children's Medical Centre, 1678 Dongfang Road, Pudong; tel: 5873 2020.

A large, modern teaching hospital built as a Sino-US joint venture.

Ruijin Hospital, 197 Ruijin No. 2 Road; tel: 6437 0045, ext 8101 (outpatients and emergencies only); 6324 0090 ext 2101 (24-hour house calls).

Large teaching hospital. The foreigners' clinic is located in Guang Ci Hospital, in the grounds.

Pharmacies

Shanghai No. 1 Dispensary, 616 Nan-jing Road East; tel: 6322 4567.

Watsons, 789 Central Huaihai Road; tel: 6474 4775.

Hours and holidays

Offices generally open Monday to Friday 9am to 6pm. Government offices are open weekdays 9am to 5pm with a one-or two-hour lunch break. Banks may stay open until 6pm or 7pm; some currency exchange desks are open around the clock, and ATMs are found everywhere.

Most large malls and department stores are generally open from 10am to 10pm, seven days a week. Smaller shops may have shorter hours. Keep in mind that most businesses are closed during Chinese New Year and other national holidays.

The list of holidays is as follows (*denotes holidays determined by the lunar calendar*):

New Year's Day: 1 Jan
Spring Festival: Jan/Feb*
Qing Ming: 4 or 5 Apr
Labour Day: 1 May
Dragon Boat Festival: June*
Mid-Autumn Festival: Sept/Oct*
National Day: 1 Oct

Note that the Spring Festival (or Chinese New Year) and National Day are week-long holidays. Schools and government offices are open the weekend before or after the one-week holiday. Spring Festival and National Day holidays signal a huge migration of travellers across China, and trains, airlines and hotels are booked out well in advance, so try to avoid travelling during these times.

ID

Visitors should carry with them a form of photo identification, such as passport, or a photocopy of it at all times.

Police in training

Internet facilities

Most hotels have either in-room WiFi or ports for high-speed internet connections. Many cafés and small restaurants offer free WiFi if you buy a coffee.

L

Language

Shanghai's official language is Mandarin *(Putonghua)*. Local residents also converse in the Shanghainese dialect. English is increasingly understood by the younger generations in downtown areas (though not by taxi drivers, so always have your destinations written in characters). Street names, public transport and utilities signage is written in Chinese and Pinyin (phonetic) or English translation, as are many restaurant menus. See page 132.

Left luggage

Luggage can be left at the airport and the train station.
Pudong International Airport: Arrivals Hall, tel: 6834 6078; Departures Hall, tel: 6834 5035.
Hongqiao Airport: Arrivals Hall, tel: 5114 4520.
Shanghai Railway Station: tel: 6354 3193.

Lost property

If you lose your passport, it's best to contact your consulate immediately. Some consulates have emergency 24-hour numbers for this. For items left in taxis, refer to the taxi receipt for the telephone number to call (the receipt also has the taxi number on it, which will help the company locate the vehicle).

M

Maps

Free tourist maps of Shanghai in English and Chinese are available at the airport, and at the concierge desks of most hotels. The maps sold at the bookshops are usually in Chinese. The *Insight Fleximap Shanghai*, which is laminated for durability, is a recommended purchase.

Media

Newspapers and magazines

Shanghai has two daily English-language newspapers. The *Shanghai Daily* (www.shanghaidaily.com) is published locally. The *China Daily* (www.chinadaily.com.cn) is the national newspaper published in Beijing. The English edition of the Chinese-language *People's Daily* is available online at http://english.peopledaily.com.cn. Foreign newspapers and magazines are only available at the city's four- and five-star hotels and foreign-language bookstores. One of the best sources is The Portman Ritz-Carlton Shanghai, which carries the *South China Morning Post, International Herald Tribune, Asian Wall Street Journal* and magazines like *Economist, Time* and *Newsweek*.

The train schedule billboard in the Southern Railway Station's main hall

Shanghai also has several free English-language publications of varying quality, most with useful listings for restaurants, bars and entertainment spots. Among the best are *Time Out* (www.timeoutshanghai.com) and *City Weekend* (www.cityweekend.com.cn). These magazines are available at many bars, restaurants and cafes around town. The online www.smartshanghai.com portal is also a useful reference.

Radio

BBC World Service is accessible on radio. English-language programming is on FM 101.7 and FM 103.7.

Television

Shanghai has two English-language TV channels. News and cultural programmes are broadcast on China Central Television (CCTV) Channel 9, while ICS is a locally produced channel with slightly more entertaining programming, including foreign movies. Most hotels will offer a range of international cable and satellite channels.

Money

The Chinese yuan (CNY) is also known as renminbi (RMB). One yuan or renminbi (colloquially called *kuai*) is divided into 10 jiao (or *mao*); one jiao is divided into 10 fen. RMB bills are issued by the Bank of China in the following denominations: one, five, 10, 20, 50 and 100. Coins come in denominations of 1 kuai, and 50 and 10 fen.

Major currencies can be changed at hotels, but you must be a registered guest, or at Bank of China and ICBC, which requires a passport. Be sure to keep the foreign exchange receipt, which is required to change your remaining renminbi back to your home currency.

International credit cards and bank cards (Cirrus, Plus, Visa, MasterCard, American Express) can be used to withdraw local currency from ATMs, which are found throughout the city. International credit cards are now accepted at major hotels and most restaurants – although many Chinese restaurants and small hotels only take cash or domestic credit cards. Cash is also king in the markets and most smaller local shops.

Locals rarely tip, and most service professionals and cab drivers don't expect tips. A service fee of 10–15 percent is added in hotels and some restaurants, and tipping for particularly good service is becoming more common at higher-end establishments and on private tours.

P

Police

Every neighbourhood has its own police station or post, often labelled in English. This is the place to report any crime, although you might have to wait for the Public Security Bureau officer in charge of foreigners to handle your case. Otherwise, contact the Public Security Bureau

Prayer flags at Jing An Temple

directly. See page 121 for a list of emergency numbers. Most public areas have roaming security guards that can help if needed.

Post

Every neighbourhood in Shanghai city has a post office, recognisable by its dark-green and yellow signage. Post offices in the busiest areas, such as Sichuan Road, Central Huaihai Road, Nanjing Road and Xujiahui, are open 14 hours a day, while the Huangpu district post office is open 24 hours a day. In addition to mailing and selling stamps, post offices also deliver local courier packages. Most large hotels will post letters to international destinations for you.

Religious services

Officially, the People's Republic encourages atheism. However, as elsewhere in China, there are Buddhist and Daoist temples and places of worship throughout the city, as well as mosques and Catholic and Protestant churches.

Buddhist and Daoist temples are well frequented by local people and are also open to visitors – some of the most popular are: City God Temple (next to Yu Garden), Jing'An Temple (1686 Nanjing Road West), Longhua Temple in the city's west (2853 Longhua Road) and the Daoist White Cloud Temple (239 Dajing Road).

Hengshan Protestant Community Church (53 Hengshan Road) in the former French Concession and Moore Memorial Baptist Church (316 Tibet Road) at People's Square host regular multi-denominational services in English and Chinese languages. Both of these churches are beautiful, historic buildings.

Muslims gather for prayers at Fuyou Road Mosque (378 Fuyou Road) and Huxi Mosque (No. 3, Lane 1328 Changde Road).

There's also an active Shanghai Jewish Centre located in Hongqiao (Shang-Mira Garden Villa 1, 1720 Hongqiao Road).

Smoking

Smoking is popular across China, and only recently have many restaurants and public spaces brought in smoke-free policies. You can still smoke in most bars, clubs and outdoor areas, and even in some restaurants.

T

Telephones

The country code for China is 86 and the city code for Shanghai is 21, or 021 when dialling from inside the country. To make an international direct dial call from Shanghai, dial the international access code: 00, followed by the country code, the area code and the local telephone number.

Local directory assistance: 114
International operator: 116

A Buddhist temple　　　　*Taikang Lu Art Street information centre*

Most public telephones in China take prepaid phone cards, which can be used for local, long-distance and international (IDD) calls. Prepaid phone cards are available in amounts of RMB 20, 30, 50 and 100.

Most mobile phone users with a roaming facility will be able to hook up with the GSM 900 local 3G or 4G networks, with the exception of those from Japan. To avoid roaming charges, get a prepaid SIM card with a local number and fixed number of minutes. Many phone providers, hotels, convenience stores and self-serve kiosks at airports sell them in denominations of RMB 100.

Time zone

The entire country operates on Beijing time, which is eight hours ahead of Greenwich Mean Time (GMT). There is no daylight saving, so the time relative to Europe and North America is one hour less advanced in the summer months. Having a single time zone in such a large country means that on the east coast the sun rises very early.

Toilets

Public toilets are plentiful in Shanghai, but toilet paper often seems to be in short supply (always carry a pack of tissues with you). Payment – usually a few jiao – is sometimes required. If you're squeamish, head for a smart hotel or shopping mall, where the public facilities are almost always user-friendly.

Tourist information

A tourist hotline (tel: 962 020) operates daily from 10am to 9pm. Information can be patchy depending on who you get on the line. Be sure to ask for an operator who speaks English. The Shanghai Tourist Information and Service Centre (http://lyw.sh.gov.cn/en) operates branches in each of Shanghai's districts, including one on the ground level of the arrival hall of Pudong International Airport, though these are geared towards Chinese-speaking travellers – the level of English spoken by the counter staff varies from one service centre to another. The service centres can book hotel rooms and tours, but of more use are the free brochures and maps they give out. Hotel concierges in five-star hotels and local tourist magazines and websites are generally the best source of current information.

Overseas tourism offices

The China National Tourism Offices abroad are useful sources for maps, brochures and travel information. Check its website at www.cnto.org. It's likely that the CNTO branches will recommend that you book your holiday packages with its affliated CITS – China International Travel Service (www.cits.net) or the CTS – China Travel Service (www.ctshk.com/english), both of which are government-run travel agencies. They handle tours, hotels, flights (international and domestic) and train

The mesmerising lights of the Bund Sight Seeing Tunnel

tickets. You can opt to use CITS or CTS agencies even before you set foot in Shanghai. Or you can fly to Shanghai and then book your trips locally, either with the CITS or CTS office in Shanghai or a privately run travel agency

Tours and guides

Various cruises on the Huangpu River and Suzhou Creek offer views of the rapidly changing cityscape along the banks of the city's two main waterways. We recommend the Huangpu River cruises for the best views of the Bund and some jaw-dropping crane action at the world's busiest container port. These leave from the Shiliupu Wharf, conveniently situated on the South Bund.

For a city tour with a difference, Shanghai Insiders (tel: 138 1761 6975; www.shanghaiinsiders.com) offers tours of the city's historic neighbourhoods in vintage motorcycle sidecars. The fabulous Changjiang 750s are replicas of Russian Ural sidecars and were formerly used by the People's Liberation Army.

You can explore Shanghai's fascinating Jewish heritage on a walking tour with Israeli documentarian and photojournalist Dvir Bar-Gal, conducted in English or Hebrew (www.shanghai-jews.com).

UnTour Shanghai runs weekly themed food tours, including 'Street Eats Breakfast' and 'Dumpling Delights', as well as private customised tours. They also arrange morning and night running tours (http://untourshanghai.com).

Transport

Shanghai has an easy-to-use and well-priced public transport system. Roads and even footpaths can be hazardous, so be careful when negotiating traffic lights and pedestrian crossings as cars seldom give way. Driving is not recommended for visitors.

Getting around

Bus: Shanghai's bus system can be confusing for visitors, and bus routes are in Chinese characters only. Taxis, which are cheap, and the metro are better options.

Metro: Thanks to a pre-Expo 2010 infrastructure boom, Shanghai has the longest metro system in the world. The city currently has 11 metro lines (with several more under construction) running all across the city from around 6am to midnight. Everything is signposted in English and Chinese, and on-train stop announcements are multilingual. Metro line 2 connects Pudong International Airport in the east with Hongqiao Airport in the far west.

Purchase a ticket at the machines in each subway station (you can press a button for English and follow the prompts). Have plenty of coinage on you, as only some machines accept notes.

Alternatively, you can purchase a stored-value Shanghai Public Transportation Card – *jiaotong yikatong* – that can be used to pay for fares on the metro, plus taxis, buses, ferries and Maglev. The

Sign for the lift to the observation deck in the World Financial Center

added bonus with the Maglev is that you won't have to produce your air ticket to get the RMB40 flyer's fare (handy when running late for your flight). The cards can be purchased at the service desk of most Shanghai metro stations with an RMB50 deposit.

Taxis: Taxis are easy to hail on the street outside rush hour – Dazhong (tel: 96822) and Jingjiang (tel: 96961) are reputable companies. Fares are cheap, straightforward and always metered, and receipts are given if requested. Flagfall is RMB 14 (RMB 18 after 11pm). Tipping is not expected. Keep the taxi receipt, which has each driver's licence number printed on it, in case you leave something behind in the car.

Arriving by air

Shanghai has two airports (www.shairport.com): Pudong International Airport (30km/19 miles east of the city – code PVG) is mainly for international flights; Hongqiao Airport (15km/9 miles west of the city – SHA) is for domestic flights and some Hong Kong, Taiwan and South Korean routes. Getting from both airports to the city is straightforward. From Pudong, official taxis into the city cost RMB 100–250, depending on your destination. The Maglev train (one way RMB 50, or RMB 40 with same-day air ticket) links with Longyang Road metro station (Line 2) in Pudong – from here, you can catch a metro or taxi to your onward destination. Ten air-conditioned airport bus routes transport passengers around the city (route details are posted in the arrivals hall). From Hongqiao, the Hongqiao Transport Hub connects Terminal 2 with metro lines 2 and 10, Hongqiao railway station and the long-distance bus station. Terminal 1 connects with metro line 10 only. Taxis are easily available and cost RMB 20–100 to downtown, depending on the final destination.

Arriving by sea

Set to become a major cruise destination, Shanghai has built the Shanghai Port International Cruise Terminal on the North Bund and another terminal on Potai Bay in Wusong Port to handle the larger vessels that are unable to pass under the Yangpu Bridge. A third terminal is located at the mouth of the Yangtze.

Arriving by train

Train services have improved dramatically in recent years, cutting travel time by hours to nearby locations such as Suzhou, Hangzhou and Nanjing. Shanghai to Beijing bullet trains depart several times a day, with a journey time of less than five hours. Most high-speed trains use Hongqiao railway station, a sparkling new hub in the city's west that integrates with the domestic airport, metro, taxis and long-distance buses.

Tickets can be purchased at the railway stations or official ticketing counters throughout the city up to 10 days ahead of the date of travel. You'll need to present your passport at the time of

The high–speed MagLev Train runs to the airport

purchase (your passport number will be printed on your ticket), as well as on the train. Most hotels can obtain train tickets for guests. If you change plans, tickets can be exchanged for a different time train up until a few minutes before the train departs by going to the correct counter in the station.

Train classes. Historically, there is no first or second class on Chinese trains, but four categories or classes: ruanwo or soft-sleeper, ruanzuo or soft-seat, yingwo or hardsleeper, and yingzuo or hard-seat. The soft-seat class is usually only available for short journeys. However, some new high-speed trains are now described as having first class, second class and even business class seats.

Long-distance trains normally only have soft-sleeper or hard-sleeper facilities. The soft-sleeper class has four-bed compartments with soft beds, and is recommended, particularly for long journeys. The hard-sleeper class has open, six-bed compartments. The beds are not really hard, but are cramped and not very comfortable. While you can reserve a place for the first three classes (you always buy a ticket with a place number), this is not always essential for the hard-seat category. There is always boiled water available on the trains. There are washrooms in the soft-sleeper and hard-sleeper classes. The toilets, regardless of which class, are usually not very hygienic, and it is a good idea to bring your own toilet paper. There are dining cars on long-distance trains.

Arriving by bus

Overland buses are the most important means of transport in many parts of China, especially where there is no railway line. In most towns and settlements there are main bus stations for overland buses. Although some rural bus journeys can be slow, China's enormously improved highway infrastructure makes major routes fast and reasonably safe. High-speed *(gaosu)* buses stick to the expressways and don't make regular stops to pick up passengers en route. There are regular breaks during bus journeys; on journeys lasting several days you will usually find simple restaurants and overnight accommodation near the bus stations. Some buses have numbered seats, but it is not usually necessary to book a ticket or seat in advance. Modern buses with air conditioning operate in tourist areas.

Car hire

You need a Chinese licence to drive in China and, besides, it's not for the faint-hearted. Dangerous driving is rampant. Avis (www.avischina.com) operates throughout Asia, offering self-drive options and cars that come with experienced drivers.

Trips out of Shanghai

The cheap option when making excursions from Shanghai is to use the special sightseeing buses that depart from several venues around town, but these are mainly used by domestic tourists

Shanghai's buses are not particularly tourist-friendly

and don't cater to foreigners (ie. people who don't speak Chinese).

Trains are one good option for independent travel to Suzhou and Hangzhou; tickets can be booked through your hotel or directly at the Shanghai Railway Station at 100 Molin Road, tel: 6317 9090.

You could also arrange to hire a private car with a driver. This option would give you the most flexibility. Some travel agencies also have English-speaking guides who will accompany you – this is useful for translation purposes, but be aware that the 'guide' may not know much about the destination itself.

Some places (like Suzhou) are standard day tours offered by travel agents. Some companies also sell a Hangzhou day trip, but this is a bit of a stretch. Ask about 2-day package tours to Hangzhou that include a night's accommodation.

Visas

Apply for visas in your home country prior to arriving in China. There are several ways of procuring one. The easiest way is to use the services of a travel agent. There will be a commission charge on top of the visa-processing fee paid to the visa office of the Chinese embassy or consulate. Individual travellers may also apply for a visa directly with the Chinese embassy or consulate in their home country. Two passport-size photos, the completed application form and the fee

are required. It takes about 7–10 working days to process your China visa, so make sure you apply for one well before your intended departure. Hong Kong is a convenient alternative. A single-entry, 30-day visa is usually provided for those with passports with a minimum of six months' validity.

Double-entry or multiple-entry visas are more expensive and more difficult to obtain.

Websites

The following websites provide a variety of information on travel-related subjects on Shanghai.

General Information
www.china.org.cn
China Foreign Ministry
www.fmprc.gov.cn/eng
Shanghai Government
www.shanghai.gov.cn
www.meet-in-shanghai.net
Hotel Bookings
www.ctrip.com
www.elong.net
Health Matters
www.worldlink-shanghai.com
Banks in Shanghai
www.sbacn.org

Weights and measures

The metric system is used across China. Traditional measurements, such as *jin* (approximately 500g) are sometimes used when buying food.

Some Mandarin phrases are useful when shopping

LANGUAGE

Mandarin is China's official language. In addition to Mandarin, known as *putong hua*, most Chinese speak local dialects. In Shanghai, the dialect is Shanghainese, or *Shanghai hua*. Written Chinese uses characters based on pictograms, which were originally pictorial representations of ideas. Some 6,000–8,000 characters are in regular use; 3,000 are sufficient for reading a newspaper. In mainland China, simplified characters are used, while Hong Kong and Taiwan use more complex characters. The standard romanisation system for Chinese characters is known as hanyu pinyin. It has been in use since 1958, and is used throughout this book.

Basic rules

Tones make it difficult for foreigners to speak Mandarin, as different tones give the same syllable completely different meanings. Take the four tones of the syllable ma for instance: the first tone má means 'mother'; the second tone má means 'hemp'; the third tone mǎ means 'horse'; and the fourth tone mà means 'to scold'. There is also a fifth, 'neutral' tone. There is a standard set of diacritical marks to indicate tones:

mā = high and even tone
má = rising tone
mǎ = falling then rising tone
mà = falling tone

Pronunciation

The pronunciation of consonants in hanyu pinyin is similar to those in English. The i after the consonants ch, c, r, sh, s, z, zh is not pronounced; it indicates that the preceding sound is lengthened.

Greetings

Hello *Nǐ hǎo* 你好
How are you? *Nǐ hǎo ma?* 你好吗?
Thank you *Xièxie* 谢谢
Goodbye *Zài jiàn* 再见
My name is... *Wǒ jiào...* 我叫…
What is your name? *Nín jiào shénme míngzi?* 您叫什么名字?
I am very happy... *Wǒ hěn gāoxìng...* 我很高兴…
Can you speak English? *Nín huì shuō Yīngyǔ ma?* 您会说英语吗?
Can you speak Chinese? *Nín huì shuō Hànyǔ ma?* 您会说汉语吗?
I cannot speak Chinese *Wǒ bù huì hànyǔ* 我不会汉语
I do not understand *Wǒ bù dǒng* 我不懂
Do you understand? *Nín dǒng ma?* 您懂吗?
Please speak a little slower *Qǐng nín shuō màn yìdiǎn* 请您说慢一点
What is this called? *Zhège jiào shénme?* 这个叫什么?
How do you say... *...Zěnme shuō?* …怎么说?
Please *Qǐng/Xièxie* 请/谢谢
Sorry *Duìbuqǐ* 对不起

A Chinese family in Century Park

Pronouns

My/mine Wǒ/wǒde 我/我的
You/yours (singular) Nǐ/nǐde 你/你的
He/his/she/hers Tā/tāde/tā/tāde 他/他的/她/她的
We/ours Wǒmen/wǒmende 我们/我们的
They/theirs Tāmen/tāmende 他们/他们的

Travel

Where is it? Zài nǎr? …在哪儿?
Do you have it here? Zhèr... yǒu ma? 这儿有…吗?
No/it's not here/there aren't any Méi yǒu 没有
Hotel Fàndiàn/bīnguǎn 饭店/宾馆
Restaurant Fànguǎn 饭馆
Bank Yínháng 银行
Post office Yóujú 邮局
Toilet Cèsuǒ 厕所
Railway station Huǒchē zhàn 火车站
Bus station Qìchē zhàn 汽车站
Embassy Dàshǐguǎn 大使馆
Consulate Lǐngshìguǎn 领事馆
Passport Hùzhào 护照
Visa Qiānzhèng 签证
Pharmacy Yàodiàn 药店
Hospital Yīyuàn 医院
Doctor Dàifu/yīshēng 大夫/医生
Translate Fānyì 翻译
Do you have...? Nín yǒu... ma? 您有…吗?
I want to go to... Wǒ yào qù... 我要去…
I want/I would like Wǒ yào/wǒ xiǎng yào 我要/我想要
I want to buy... Wǒ xiǎng mǎi... 我想买…

Shopping

How much does it cost? Zhège duōshǎo qián? 这个多少钱?
Too expensive, thank you Tài guì le, xièxie 太贵了，谢谢

Money, hotels, transport, communications

Money Qián 钱
Credit card Xìnyòngkǎ 信用卡
Foreign currency Wàihuìquàn 外汇券
Where can I change money? Zài nǎr kěyǐ huàn qián? 在哪儿可以换钱?
What is the exchange rate? Bǐjià shì duōshǎo? 比价是多少?
We want to stay for one (two/three) nights Wǒmen xiǎng zhù yì tiān (liǎng/sān) tiān 我们想住一(两，三)天
How much is the room per day? Fángjiān duōshǎo qián yì tiān? 房间多少钱一天?
Room number Fángjiān hàomǎ 房间号码
Reception Qiántái/fúwùtái 前台/服务台
Key Yàoshi 钥匙
Luggage Xíngli 行李
Airport Fēijīchǎng 飞机场
Bus Gōnggòng qìchē 公共汽车
Taxi Chūzū qìchē 出租汽车
Bicycle Zìxíngchē 自行车
Telephone Diànhuà 电话
Use the Internet Shàngwǎng 上网

Time

When? Shénme shíhou? 什么时候?
What time is it now? Xiànzàijǐ diǎn zhōng? 现在几点钟?
How long? Duōcháng shíjiān? 多长时间?

Early morning/morning *Zǎoshàng/ shàngwǔ* 早上/上午

Midday/afternoon/evening *Zhōngwǔ/ xiàwǔ/wǎnshang* 中午/下午/晚上

Yesterday/today/tomorrow *Zuótiān/ jīntiān/míngtiān* 昨天/今天/明天

Hour/day/week/month *Xiǎoshí/tiān/ xīngqī/yuè* 小时/天/星期/月

Eating out

Waiter/waitress *Fúwùyuán/xiǎojiě* 服务员/小姐

Menu *Càidān* 菜单

Chopsticks *Kuàizi* 筷子

Knife *Dāozi* 刀子

Fork *Chāzi* 叉子

Spoon *Sháozi* 勺子

I am a vegetarian *Wǒ shì chī sù de rén* 我是吃素的人

Beer *Píjiǔ* 啤酒

Red/white wine *Hóng/bái pú táo jiǔ* 红/白葡萄酒

Green/black tea *Lǜchá/hóngchá* 绿茶/红茶

Coffee *Kāfēi* 咖啡

Beef/pork/lamb/chicken *Niúròu/ zhūròu/yángròu/jīròu* 牛肉/猪肉/羊肉/鸡肉

Spicy/sweet/sour/salty *Là/tián/suān/ xián* 辣/甜/酸/咸

Can we have the bill, please *Qǐng jié zhàng/mǎidān* 请结帐/买单

Numbers

One/two/three/four/five *Yī/ér/sān/ sì/wǔ* 一/二/三/四/五

Six/seven/eight/nine/ten *Liù/qī/bā/ jiǔ/shí* 六/七/八/九/十

Eleven/twelve/twenty/thirty/forty *Shíyī/shíèr/érshí/sānshí/sìshí* 十一/十二/二十/三十/四十

Fifty/sixty/seventy/eighty/ninety *Wǔshí/liùshí/qīshí/bāshí/jiǔshí* 五十/六十/七十/八十/九十

One hundred *Yībǎi* 一百

One thousand *Yìqiān* 一千

Place names

Bank of China 中国银行 Zhongguo Yin-hang

Century Park 世纪公园 Shiji Gongyuan

Chenxiangge Nunnery 沉香阁 Chenxiang Ge

China Art Palace 中华艺术宫 Zhonghua Yishu Gong

City God Temple 城隍庙 Cheng Huang Miao

Confucius Temple 文庙 Wen Miao

Customs House 海关大楼 Haiguan Dalou

Dongtai Road Antiques Market 东台路古玩市场 Dongtai Lu Guwan Shichang

Doulun Lu Cultural Celebrity St Fa Zang Temple 多伦路文化街法藏讲寺 Duolun Lu Wenhua Jie Fazang Jiang Si

Former residence of Lu Xun 鲁迅故居 Luxun Guju

Former residence of Sun Yat-sen 孙中山故居 Sun Zhongshan Guju

Former residence of Zhou en-lai 周公馆 Zhou Gonguan

Fuxing Park 复兴公园 Fuxing Gongyuan

Fuyou Road Mosque 福佑路清真寺 Fuyou Lu Qingzhen Si

Hengshan Moller Villa 衡山马勒别墅 Hengshan Male Bieshu

Many street signs are in both Mandarin and English

Huangpu Park 黄浦公园 Huangpu Gongyuan

Huxinting Teahouse 湖心亭 Huxin Ting

Jade Buddha Temple 玉佛寺 Yufo Si

Jing An Park 静安公园 Jing'an Gongyuan

Jing An Si 静安寺 Jing'an Si

Jinmao Tower 金贸大厦 Jin Mao Dasha

Longhua Pagoda and Temple 龙华塔，龙华庙 Longhua Ta, Longhua Miao

Lu Xun Memorial Hall 鲁迅纪念馆 Luxun Jinianguan

Lu Xun Park 鲁迅公园 Luxun Gongyuan

M Glamour 魅力酒吧 Meili Jiuba

Moore Memorial Church 摩恩堂 Mo'en Tang

Municipal Children's Palace 上海少年宫 Shanghai Shaonian Gong

Museum of Contemporary Art 上海当代艺术馆 Shanghai Dangdai Yishuguan

Oriental Arts Centre 东方艺术中心 Dongfang Yishu Zhongxin

Oriental Pearl Tower 东方明珠 Dongfang Mingzhu

People's Park 人民公园 Renmin Gongyuan

Power Station of Art 当代艺术博物馆 Dandai Yishu Bowuguan

Qinci Yangdian Temple 钦赐仰殿道观 Qinci Yangdian Daoguan

Rockbund Art Museum 上海外滩美术馆 Shanghai Waitan Meishuguan

Ohel Rachel Synagogue 犹太教堂 Youtai Jiaotang

Shanghai Arts & Crafts 上海工艺美术博物馆 Shanghai Gongyi Museum Meishu Bowuguan

Shanghai Botanical Gardens 上海植物园 Shanghai Zhiwuyuan

Shanghai Culture Square 上海文化广 Shanghai Wenhua Guangchang

Shanghai Concert Hall 上海音乐厅 Shanghai Yinyue Ting

Shanghai Exhibition Centre 上海展览馆 Shanghai Zhanlanguan

Shanghai Grand Theatre 上海大剧院 Shanghai Da Juyuan

Shanghai Jewish Refugees 犹太难民在上海纪念馆 Youtai Nanmin Zai Museum Shanghai Jinianguan

Shanghai Municipal History 上海历史博物馆 Shanghai Lishi Bowuguan Museum

Shanghai Museum 上海博物馆 Shanghai Bowuguan

Shanghai Ocean Aquarium 上海海洋水族馆 Shanghai Haiyang Shuizuguan

Shanghai Postal Museum 上海邮政博物馆 Shanghai Youzheng Bowuguan

Shanghai Pudong Development Bank 上海浦发银行 Shanghai Pufa Yinhang

Shanghai Science & Technology Museum 上海科技馆 Shanghai Keji Guan

Shanghai Tower 上海中心大厦 Shanghai Zhongxin Dasha

Shanghai World Financial 上海国际金融中心 Shanghai Guoji Jinrong Centre Zhongxin

Waibaidu Bridge 外白渡桥 Waibaidu Qiao

Wanshang Bird and Flower Market 万商花鸟市场 Wanshang Huaniao Shichang

Xiahai Temple 下海庙 Xiahai Miao

Xujiahui Cathedral 徐家汇教堂 Xujiahui Jiaotang

LUXUN NATIVE PLACE

BOOKS AND FILM

Shanghai's early 20th century cultural heyday saw Chinese and foreign directors and writers take inspiration from its incorrigible joie de vivre. After Mao's 1949 Communist Revolution, the arts languished until a curious 1990s generation of creative talents began exploring the complexities of Chinese society as the country opened up to the world.

Before 1949, Shanghai was the centre of Chinese cinema, where successful studios, such as Mingxing, Lianhua and Tianyi, produced hundreds of movies aimed at an avid local audience. The Shanghai film industry endured until 1949, with Crows and Sparrows being the most searing portrait of life in Nationalist China.

Shanghai's literary and cinematic ambitions dovetailed in the 1920s, when Lu Xun, one of China's most celebrated novelists, convened regular meetings for forward-thinking authors and philosophers in cafés near his home in Hongkou (see page 58). Mirroring the cinematic arts, Shanghai's authorial talents remained subdued until the late 1990s, when fascinating accounts of the city began to be penned.

Books

The True Story of Ah Q, Lu Xun (1922). Regarded as the father of modern Chinese literature, Shanghai-born Lu Xun's gripping tale is essential for understanding the nation's complex contemporary culture.

Western Architecture in Shanghai: A Last Look, Tess Johnston and Deke Erh (2004). Beautifully photographed coffee-table tome chronicling the origins and architects of Shanghai's rich portfolio of early 20th century villas, mansions and apartment buildings.

Carl Crow – A Tough Old China Hand, Paul French (2006). Fascinating story of an American journalist, ad-man and business networker who became a ubiquitous feature of Shanghai society during the 1920s and 30s.

Inspector Chen Series, Qiu Xiaolong. This 'page-turner' mystery series follows the Chinese poetry-loving Inspector Chen, who trails his suspects through gritty Shanghai streets. *Death of a Red Heroine* and *When Red is Black* are two of the best tales.

The Valley of Amazement, Amy Tan (2013). This tale of several women's intertwined fates begins in a Shanghai courtesan house as the Qing dynasty is being overthrown.

Old Shanghai: Gangsters in Paradise, Lynn Pan (1984). Historian Lynn Pan explores Shanghai's shady underworld characters of the late 19th and early 20th centuries, who influenced the development of the city.

Life and Death in Shanghai, Nien Cheng (1995). A chilling insight into life

Lu Xun is revered as one of China's improtant thinkers and writers

and society during Mao's Cultural Revolution, when the author was accused of espionage and jailed.

Man's Fate, André Malraux (1990). Haunting novel about Shanghai's 'White Terror' in 1927 when Chiang Kai-shek and the Green Gang massacred the city's communists.

The Boat to Redemption, Su Tong (2011). Winner of the 2009 Man Asian Literary Prize, Su Tong grew up in neighbouring Suzhou. This political fable tells of a disgraced Party official who starts a new life with his teenage son on a barge fleet.

Phantom Shanghai, Greg Girad (2007). Peerless photographic collection of Shanghai's old neighbourhoods and buildings that have been dismantled and replaced by the city's new vision of cosmopolitan living.

Five Star Billionaire, Tash Aw (2013). Set in today's Shanghai, this sharp allegory of modern life charts the stories of five Malaysians magnetised by the allure of China's wealthiest, most hedonistic city.

Film

Shanghai Express (1932). Set on an express train between Beijing and Shanghai as war wages outside. Director Josef von Sternberg's muse, Marlene Dietrich, smoulders as an infamous courtesan.

Shanghai Gesture (1941). Mother Gin Sling runs her infamous joint with the help of Victor Mature's Doctor Omar, corrupting Gene Tierney in the back-streets of old Shanghai.

Empire of the Sun (1987). Steven Spielberg's gripping movie, based on a World War II memoir by J.G. Ballard about a teenage boy abandoned in Shanghai during the Japanese occupation, was the first Western film shot in Shanghai since Mao's 1949 Communist Revolution.

Shanghai Triad (1995). Zhang Yimou reimagined the 1930s underworld with China's first superstar actress Gong Li giving a stellar performance as a gangster's moll.

Suzhou River (2000). This film noir directed by Shanghai native Lou Ye weaves a love story against a backdrop of Shanghai's emergent, gritty urban experience, starring then-unknown actress Zhou Xun, who is now a Chinese movie megastar.

Lust, Caution (2007) Espionage thriller by Taiwanese-born director Ang Lee *(Life of Pi)* based on a novella by Eileen Chang about a group of university students who plot to assassinate a government agent during the Japanese wartime occupation of Shanghai.

Skyfall (2012) The 23rd James Bond movie brought 007 to Shanghai, where the futuristic skyline and elevated highways made a star appearance.

Gone With the Bullets (2014) Jiang Wen's gritty follow-up to *Let the Bullets Fly* is set in 1920s Shanghai and is a based on the true story of a beauty pageant patronised by the city's glamorous elite that triggered a succession of dramatic and tragic events.

ABOUT THIS BOOK

This *Explore Guide* has been produced by the editors of Insight Guides, whose books have set the standard for visual travel guides since 1970. With top-quality photography and authoritative recommendations, these guidebooks bring you the very best routes and itineraries in the world's most exciting destinations.

BEST ROUTES

The routes in the book provide something to suit all budgets, tastes and trip lengths. As well as covering the destination's many classic attractions, the itineraries track lesser-known sights, and there are also excursions for those who want to extend their visit outside the city. The routes embrace a range of interests, so whether you are an art fan, a gourmet, a history buff or have kids to entertain, you will find an option to suit.

We recommend reading the whole of a route before setting out. This should help you to familiarise yourself with it and enable you to plan where to stop for refreshments – options are shown in the 'Food and Drink' box at the end of each tour.

For our pick of the tours by theme, consult Recommended Routes for… (see pages 4–5).

INTRODUCTION

The routes are set in context by this introductory section, giving an overview of the destination to set the scene, plus background information on food and drink, shopping and more, while a succinct history timeline highlights the key events over the centuries.

DIRECTORY

Also supporting the routes is a Directory chapter, with a clearly organised A–Z of practical information, our pick of where to stay while you are there and select restaurant listings; these eateries complement the more low-key cafés and restaurants that feature within the routes and are intended to offer a wider choice for evening dining. Also included here are some nightlife listings, plus a handy language guide and our recommendations for books and films about the destination.

ABOUT THE AUTHORS

After a career spent touring the world as a professional classical ballerina, Amy Fabris-Shi is now enjoying the realm of lifestyle and travel writing. Born in Sydney and based in Shanghai for the past eight years, Amy worked as a magazine editor before co-founding Scribes of the Orient, specialising in China-based publishing and communications services. She is China Correspondent for travel trade publications TTG Asia and TTG MICE and her articles on lifestyle, design and travel regularly appear in a wide range of books and magazines. This book contains content originally written by author Tina Kanagaratnam, who has lived in Shanghai since 1997, where she is the CEO for communications consulting firm AsiaMedia

CONTACT THE EDITORS

We hope you find this Explore Guide useful, interesting and a pleasure to read. If you have any questions or feedback on the text, pictures or maps, please do let us know. If you have noticed any errors or outdated facts, or have suggestions for places to include on the routes, we would be delighted to hear from you. Please drop us an email at insight@apaguide.co.uk. Thanks!

CREDITS

Explore Shanghai
Contributors: Amy Fabris-Shi
Commissioning Editor: Sarah Clark
Series Editor: Sarah Clark
Pictures/Art: Tom Smyth/Shahid Mahmood
Map Production: originial cartography
Stephen Ramsay, updated by Apa
Cartography Department
Production: Tynan Dean and Rebeka Davies
Photo credits: Alamy 82, 102, 136/137;
Alex Havret/Apa Publications 14; Bigstock
63; Corbis 81; David Shen Kai/Apa Publications 1, 2MC, 2MR, 2MC, 4BC, 5T, 5MR,
5M, 6MC, 6MR, 9L, 10/11, 11, 12/13,
13, 15, 16, 19, 25, 26MC, 26ML, 26/27T,
28/29, 30, 31, 30/31, 34, 36, 36/37,
38, 40, 40/41, 43, 44, 45, 44/45, 46, 48,
50, 50/51, 52, 53, 54, 55, 54/55, 56, 57,
58, 58/59, 59, 60, 61, 62, 65, 66, 66/67,
68, 68/69, 69, 74, 74/75, 76, 84, 85, 86,
86/87, 88, 90, 90/91, 91, 92ML, 92MC,
92/93T, 95, 100/101, 106, 107, 109, 116,
118/119, 120, 124, 126, 126/127, 127,
132, 132/133; Dreamstime 8, 20, 22/23,
23, 29, 32, 34/35, 60/61, 70, 78, 78/79,
80, 82/83, 84/85, 88/89, 99, 100, 104,
104/105, 118; iStockphoto 22, 28, 35L,
70/71, 73L, 92MR, 102/103; Leonardo
94, 96, 96/97, 98/99; Mary Evans Picture
Library 24, 24/25; Photoshot 6/7T, 20/21;
Richard and Abe Nowitz/Apa Pubications
14/15; Ritz-Carlton 112, 112/113, 113;
Ryan Pyle/Apa Publications 2ML, 2MR,
2ML, 2/3T, 4TL, 4MC, 4ML, 5MR, 6ML,
6MR, 6MC, 6ML, 8/9, 10, 12, 16/17, 17,
18, 18/19, 26ML, 26MR, 26MC, 26MR,
32/33, 38/39, 39, 42, 42/43, 46/47, 47,
48/49, 49, 51, 52/53, 56/57, 64, 64/65,
72, 72/73, 76/77, 77, 92MR, 92MC,
92ML, 94/95, 106/107, 108, 108/109,
110, 110/111, 114, 114/115, 116/117,
117, 120/121, 122, 122/123, 123,
124/125, 128, 128/129, 130, 130/131,
134/135; Starwood 98
Cover credits: Front Cover Main: View
of the Oriental Pearl TV Tower and the
Shanghai International Convention Centre,
4Corners Images; **Front Cover BL:** Golden

Buddha Statues at the Longhua Temple,
Ryan Pyle/Apa Publications; **Back Cover:**
(Left) West Lake Hangzhou, *David Shen Kai/
Apa Publications*; (Right): Xin Tian di Shang-
hai, *David Shen Kai/Apa Publications*

Printed by CTPS – China
© 2014 Apa Publications (UK) Ltd
All Rights Reserved
First Edition 2014

DISTRIBUTION

Worldwide: APA Publications GmbH & Co.
Verlag KG (Singapore branch)
7030 Ang Mo Kio Ave 5, 08-65
Northstar @ AMK, Singapore 569880
Email: apasin@singnet.com.sg
UK and Ireland: Dorling Kindersley Ltd
(a Penguin Company)
80 Strand, London, WC2R 0RL, UK
Email: sales@uk.dk.com
US: Ingram Publisher Services
One Ingram Blvd, PO Box 3006, La Vergne,
TN 37086-1986
Email: ips@ingramcontent.com
Australia and New Zealand: Woodslane
10 Apollo St, Warriewood NSW 2102,
Australia
Email: info@woodslane.com.au

INDEX

MAP LEGEND

● Start of tour

→ Tour & route direction

❶ Recommended sight

❷ Recommended
   restaurant/café

★ Place of interest
❶ Tourist information
𝟏 Statue/monument
🚌 Main bus station
Ⓢ Metro station
✚ Church
🛕ψ🏯 Buddhist, Chinese,
   Hindu temple

☐ Park
☐ Important building
☐ Hotel
☐ Transport hub
☐ Shop / market
☐ Pedestrian area
☐ Urban area

INSIGHT GUIDES

INSPIRING YOUR NEXT ADVENTURE

Insight Guides offers you a range of travel guides
to match your needs. Whether you are looking for
inspiration for planning a trip, cultural information,
walks and tours, great listings, or practical advice, we
have a product to suit you.